Bruce L. Benson

PRIVATIZATION IN CRIMINAL JUSTICE

The INDEPENDENT INSTITUTE

INDEPENDENT POLICY REPORT

BJL 2897-9/1

Independent Policy Reports are published by The Independent Institute, a non-profit, non-partisan, scholarly research and educational organization that sponsors comprehensive studies on the political economy of critical social and economic issues. Nothing herein should be construed as necessarily reflecting the views of the Institute or as an attempt to aid or hinder the passage of any bill before Congress. Address publisher inquiries to The Independent Institute, 134 Ninety-Eighth Avenue, Oakland, CA 94603, telephone (510) 632-1366, fax (510) 568-6040, E-mail: info@independent.org. Web site: http://www.independent.org.

Copyright ©1996 The Independent Institute

ISBN 0-945999-54-2

Privatization in Criminal Justice

Bruce L. Benson

About 20 years ago, a National Advisory Commission on Criminal Justice Standards and Goals report (1976) began with a description of the crime problem that is echoed everywhere today, and its conclusions are now even more relevant:

> [T]his country has become the unwilling victim of a crime epidemic. The present seriousness of the disease has outstripped even the most pessimistic prognosis. Coupled with a steadily rising numerical frequency of crimes is a savage viciousness that has rendered the American public almost immune from further shock...

> In a valiant but vain attempt to stem this massive tide of criminality, government officials, scholars, politicians, and a vast array of other professionals have responded with plans, programs, and projects all designed to reduce crime...[A]lthough many of these programs were improvements over outdated practices, crime, the cost of crime, the damages from crime, and the fear of crime continued to increase.

Bruce L. Benson is Distinguished Research Professor in the Department of Economics at Florida State University and a Reasearch Fellow for the Independent Institute. Portions of this report are drawn from the author's book *The Enterprise of Law: Justice Without the State.*

One massive resource...has not been tapped by governments in the fight against criminality. The private security industry...offers a potential for coping with crime that can not be equaled by any other remedy....[T]he private security professional may be the only person in this society who has the knowledge to effectively prevent crime.

This report had no noticeable impact on crime policy. In fact, a 1985 National Institute of Justice report (Cunningham and Taylor 1985, 1-3) explains that, despite continual increases in taxpayer dollars spent on the criminal justice system as new programs and projects are hatched by public officials, "neither local, State, nor Federal resources had seriously affected the problem of crime"; and yet, still "conspicuously absent from...crime prevention programs...is the input of the private security industry."

The security industry is actually only one component of the largely unappreciated but vital private-sector involvement in crime control. Indeed, the crime policy question should be framed more broadly than the typical "what can government do to reduce crime?" Instead, we should be asking "what is the most cost-effective way to reduce crime?" It will be contended below that the answer must include a significant increase in private sector involvement. The primary purpose of this report is to suggest ways of achieving this. To frame these suggestions, however, the wide variety of current private-sector criminal justice activities will be discussed first.

The first section examines contracting out for prisons, policing, and other criminal justice functions generally performed by the government, while the next section focuses on the benefits and pitfalls of such contracting. The section on "private inputs" explores the reasons for the low level of crucial private-sector involvement in the production of arrests and prosecutions, reasons that also explain widespread private investments in protection, detailed in the next section and in the section on "private justice." The significant benefits and alleged costs of privatization in crime control and justice are then examined, and policy alternatives are explored in the final section.

PARTIAL PRIVATIZATION: CONTRACTING OUT IN CRIMINAL JUSTICE

Virtually everything governments do, including police, security, jails, prisons, and court-related services, is being contracted out somewhere in the United States,

Contracting for Police Services

A 1972 survey found no city contracting directly with a private firm for all police services, and less than 1 percent of cities were found to dealing with private firms for subservice police functions (Fisk et al. 1978, 33). This has changed dramatically. Today, local governments contract with private firms for a wide array of traditional police functions, particularly in the area of "police support" services, including accounting, maintenance, communications, data processing, the towing of illegally parked cars, fingerprinting prisoners, conducting background checks on job applicants, and directing traffic (Chaiken and Chaiken 1987, 1–3). Security firms also provide guards for public buildings, sports arenas, and other public facilities. Indeed, while manufacturing firms and retailers rank first and second in contracting with security firms, government agencies rank third (Chaiken and Chaiken 1987, 3).

Wackenhut Services, Inc., for example, has a long record of contracting with governments. It provides the entire police force for the Energy Research and Development Administration's 1,600-square-mile Nevada nuclear test site and for the Kennedy Space Center in Florida (Poole 1978, 41–42). The state of Florida contracted with Wackenhut for security guards at all its highway rest stops after a 1993 rest-stop murder of a tourist. This firm also provides security for courthouses in Texas and Florida, patrols for the Miami Downtown Development Authority, guards for the Miami Metro Rail and the Tri-Rail from West Palm Beach to Dade County, complete police services for the Tampa Airport, predeparture security for many other airports, and so on (Reynolds 1994, 11). Thousands of firms offer similar services.

A small number of local governments have actually

contracted for complete police services.[1] For instance, in 1975, Oro Valley, Arizona, arranged such a contract with Rural/Metro Fire Department, Inc. (Gage 1982, 25), although the arrangement was challenged by the Arizona Law Enforcement Officers Advisory Council, which argued that under Arizona law, an employee of a private firm could not be a police officer. Rural/Metro could not bear the high court fees required to fight the challenge, so in 1977, the arrangement was ended. Several other contracts like this have been written elsewhere, however. Guardsmark, Inc., began providing full police services to Buffalo Creek, West Virginia, in 1976 (Poole 1978, 42). Wackenhut had contracts with three separate Florida jurisdictions in 1980 and had proposals pending with 20 communities in 1985 (Cunningham and Taylor 1985, 47), and Reminderville, Ohio, contracted with Corporate Security, Inc. in 1981 (Gage 1982, 24). Similarly, after the entire police force of Sussex, New Jersey, was dismissed due to a drug scandal, the community contracted with Executive Security & Investigations Services, Inc. (*New York Times*, July 13, 1993). Contracting for all police services is, therefore, increasingly being recognized as a serious alternative.

Contracting for Corrections

Almost every aspect of corrections in publicly run facilities, including food services, counseling, industrial programs, maintenance, security, education, and vocational training, is under contract with private firms on a piecemeal basis (Logan and Rausch 1985, 307). In addition, contracting out for provision and management of entire correctional facilities is common. The Federal Bureau of Prisons contracts out all of its halfway-house operations (Poole 1983, 1), for instance, and in 1985, 32 states had nonsecure, community-based facilities (e.g., halfway houses, group homes, community treatment centers) under contract (Mullen et al. 1985, 56–68). In that same year, approximately 34,080 juvenile offenders were held in nearly 1,996 privately run facilities nationwide. The first privately operated high-security institution in recent history was an

---

1. Furthermore, this practice is quite common in Switzerland, for example, where one firm, Secuitas, provides police services for more than 30 Swiss villages and townships (Reynolds 1994).

intensive-treatment unit for juveniles at Weaverville, Pennsylvania, that RCA began running in 1975; by 1983, there were 73 privately provided secure juvenile facilities (Logan and Rausch 1985, 307).

Privatization of major adult detention facilities did not begin until the early 1980s when Behavioral Systems Southwest provided a minimum-security Immigration and Naturalization Service prison (Fixler 1984, 2). This market is expanding rapidly. Corrections Corporation of America, Inc. (CCA), formed in 1983, is now the largest private supplier of secure adult facilities, with a rated capacity of 9,045 in operation or under contractual construction in 1992 (*Corrections Today*, December 1992, 14). In 1988, CCA received a contract from New Mexico to design, finance, construct, and operate a prison for all of the state's female felons, becoming the first private minimum-through-maximum-security state prison in recent history. Contracting firms increased from 17 to 21 between 1992 and 1993, as the number of facilities increased by 14.5 percent: on June 30, 1993, 20,698 adults were being held in 65 private facilities, giving private firms a 1.5 percent "market share" of adult prisons (Reynolds 1994, 32).

Contracting for Court-Related Services

Contracting for judges is not developing, although even more complete privatization (e.g., arbitration, for-profit courts and other less formal ways of imposing private sanctions) is very widespread (see the section on "private justice"). Contracting with private firms for all "public defender" services has become the predominant system in some states, such as North Dakota, and contracts for all cases that a public defender's office cannot handle exist in about 10 percent of the nation's counties (Schulhofer and Friedman 1993, 89). Furthermore, about 60 percent of the nation's counties assign a private attorney on a case-by-case basis to defend accused criminals who cannot pay (Schulhofer and Friedman 1993, 92). Prosecution by private attorneys also is occasionally practiced (Reynolds 1994, 30).

POTENTIAL BENEFITS AND PITFALLS OF
CONTRACTING OUT IN CRIMINAL JUSTICE

The Institute for Local Self Government dismissed contracting out for police services as unfeasible, because "there are no secret methods, known only to the private sector, of running an entire police department" (quoted in Poole 1983, 10). But the relevant issue is not knowledge; it is *incentives* (Fitch 1974, 509)!

Reduced Costs Through Contracting

As the president of Arizona's Rural/Metro Fire Department, Inc., noted: "We have the greatest incentive in the world to innovate, to pioneer, to analyze every little step. Sheer survival" (quoted in Poole 1978, 28). When firms compete every year or two to renew their contracts, they must look for ways to keep costs (and, therefore, prices) lower than their potential competitors. And a firm that can offer better services than competitors at similar costs will be in a strong position for contract renewal and for obtaining new contracts elsewhere. Therefore, they have very strong incentives to monitor costs, avoid unnecessarily expensive means of production, and discover lower-cost means of producing the desired output.

Police chiefs and corrections officials reap no special reward (e.g., profit) by successfully producing quality services at the lowest possible cost. Therefore, they have much weaker incentives to be concerned about production costs. This does not imply that they will be completely ambivalent to costs; it simply means that they are likely to make a relatively smaller effort at monitoring employees to check on wasted time and resources, and likely to be less motivated to search for more efficient production methods. Even public managers who ignore the incentives and act like profit maximizers may not be effective, given the organizational inflexibility inherent in the civil service system, which prevents management from disciplining inefficient employees unless their behavior is extreme (Savas 1974, 492). Lateral movement to adjust manpower needs in the face of changing demands is also virtually impossible, as is hiring at any but the lowest grades. Thus, the major source of savings from contracting out is labor costs. CCA reported that because they are not restricted by civil service rules, they pay less in wages, and that labor savings also arise through designing facilities so that a smaller staff is needed.

A number of evaluation studies of contract prisons have been performed. They regularly find savings of 20 percent from construction costs and 5 to 15 percent from private management relative to the costs of comparable public facilities (Logan and McGriff 1989; Logan 1990; Bowman et al. 1993). Unfortunately, no evaluations of contract policing have been done to compare their costs with public police forces, although there is anecdotal evidence of similar savings (Gage 1982; Benson 1990, 186), and in every other area that has been evaluated (e.g., fire protection, garbage collection, data processing, maintenance), contracting out produced savings of from 10 to 50 percent (Poole 1978, 27).

Achieving Flexibility Through Contracting

The Federal Bureau of Prisons contracted for its new medium-security facility in 1985, because, as a bureau spokesman noted (Krajick 1984b, 23):

> Rather than build our own institution for something that might be a temporary phenomenon, we decided not to take the risk. Besides it takes two or three years for us to site and build a place. This is an immediate need, which the private sector has offered to fill. If at some point we don't need the place anymore, we can terminate the contract.

The general inability of governments to quickly respond to changing needs has been an important spur for contracting out (Fitch 1974, 502). Further, it is much more difficult to "terminate the contract" with public-employee unions or close public facilities than it is to end private contracts (Wynne 1978, 198–228).

Enhanced Quality Through Contracting

Critics have raised concerns about the quality of government services purchased from the private sector. Mark Cunniff, director of the National Association of Criminal Justice Planners, expects private firms that provide prisons to cut costs by cutting back on services, for instance, making the prison situation worse than it already is (Krajick 1984b, 27). There are at least two major flaws in such arguments. First, private firms selling services to government units have reputations to maintain so that they can retain contracts and continue to attract new customers. Indeed, a survey of 89 municipal governments regarding contracting out found that the most frequently applied criteria used for awarding large contracts was *documented past performance* (Florestano and Gordon 1980, 32).

Second, in a competitive market, the quality of the outcome depends more on demand-side incentives than supply-side incentives. If the government attempts to get a bargain by limiting payments too much (e.g., relative to the costs of production for the services by a public bureau), quality can fall, but private providers who simply must cut costs relative to public production generally simultaneously enhance quality. For instance, independent observers who monitor private prisons generally praise their operations (Benson 1990, 190–91; Logan 1992). In a comparison of privately and publicly operated corrections facilities in Massachusetts and Kentucky, both staff and inmates rated the services and programs in the private prisons higher than their counterparts in publicly operated institutions; and the private facilities had lower escape rates and fewer inmate disturbances (Joel 1993). The same conclusion appears to apply for contract policing (Gage 1982; Benson 1990, 186).

On the other hand, the quality of contract public-defender services has been questioned, at least from the perspective of the criminal defendant (Wilson 1982). Public defenders generally have strong incentives to move cases quickly, thus encouraging plea bargaining perhaps even to the degree of not fully or accurately informing defendants of their options or the probability of success at trial (Schulhofer 1988; Rasmussen and Benson 1994a, 155–64). Contracting out for defense attorney services does not alter these incentives if the contracted fee is based on volume of cases handled, or if the contract requires the provider to handle all cases of a particular type (Schulhofer and Friedman 1993, 91). However, Schulhofer and Friedman (1993, 96–122) explain that contracting out is much more likely to produce quality defense from a defendant's perspective than expanding the public-defender bureaucracy. This might be achieved by a voucher system, for instance, wherein indigent defendants are free to contract with their own attorneys (Schulhofer and Friedman 1993, 122). The point is that "quality" may depend on perspective, and contracts can be adjusted to create whatever level and definition of quality the payers want. Thus, the quality of services provided through contracting remains predominantly a function of the demand side of the process. This is, in fact, the problem with contracting out.

Pitfalls in Contracting Out

The lower costs of prisons and policing that can result from contracting out could make "criminalization" even more attractive as a "solution" to political problems. If Hitler had contracted out the rounding up and extermination of Jews, it might have been accomplished at a lower cost, but the fact that more of these politically defined "criminals" could have been exterminated more "efficiently" does not mean that contracting out that process would have been desirable. Similarly, many of the problems now facing the criminal justice system arise, at least in part, because of the criminalization of the sale and consumption of various drugs (Benson 1994b; Rasmussen and Benson 1994a; Benson and Rasmussen 1994), a problem that apparently could be more effectively handled with treatment-based rather than punishment-based programs (Rasmussen and Benson 1994b). But if contracting lowers the cost of punishment, treatment is less likely to be considered. This is not an indictment of contracting out per se, of course (indeed, treatment-based programs are also contracted out). However, even for desirable criminal justice functions, the benefits of contracting out will be marginal at best because of the remaining problems that exist in criminal justice (Benson 1994b; Rasmussen and Benson 1994a, 1994b).

As Krajick (1984b, 23) warned: "Efficient as these profit-making concerns may be, the institutions they run are bound to reflect to some extent the aims, limitations, and perhaps abuses of the government systems of which they become a part." Consider the belief that "one efficient firm and a knowledgeable government official can reach an agreement to provide services at a cost no higher than it would be if ten suppliers were bidding" (Fisk et al. 1978, 5). This bureaucratic attitude could quickly destroy the effectiveness of the contracting process. After all, competition is the automatic safeguard of the market process that regulates self-interested behavior.[2] When a single private firm is given a contract with no fear of future competition, it begins to act like a monopolist, not an efficient competitor.

The government raises significant barriers to competition in contracting. "The high cost of obtaining government contracts ...and other costs frequently imposed by government regulation, and the problems raised by zealous auditors make government contracting for the typical small firm, and for many large firms a chancy business. The risks impel many firms to limit the amount of government business they seek" (Fitch 1974, 518). The excuse for heavy regulation is supposedly to prevent dishonest private firms from providing poor services, but a sufficiently competitive contracting process would do precisely that, as competitors monitor each other in hopes of spotting inefficiencies or abuses that will allow them to offer a superior contract.

Many critics fear "that contract prisons will generate the same kinds of scandals as contract nursing homes, which despite numerous inspectors and standards have still frequently become substandard facilities" (Krajick 1984a, 27). Such concerns may not be unwarranted. After all, as Fitch (1974, 517) noted, many regulations "have the effect of putting a greater strain on honest firms than on dishonest firms, which can often find some way of beating the regulation, if only by buying cooperation of government contracting officers." This brings us to another potential barrier to competition: political corruption becomes possible when government officials control the allocation of valuable rights (Benson 1981).

Not surprisingly, "contracts are one of the most common and lucrative sources of corruption in government" (Fitch 1974, 517).

---

2. Fisk et al. (1978: 8) worried that reasonable levels of competition might not exist in the contracting process because "few, if any, private firms exist to provide [certain services]...in most places," but if the market is attractive (profitable) many firms will try to enter. Control Data Corporation, a conglomerate that deals mainly in computers, has bid for corrections contracts, for instance (Krajick 1984b: 24). CCA, founded by Thomas Beasley and backed by the Massey Burch Investment Group, also started Hospital Corporation of America. Beasley had no prison management experience, but CCA is run "with large purchase orders and centralized accounting and management, and by hiring experienced professionals [including a former commissioner of corrections from Arkansas and Virginia, and a retired chairman of the U.S. Parole Commission] from public agencies to run the day-to-day affairs of the institutions" (Krajick 1984b: 23).

In such cases, critics of contracting out for government services may be absolutely right when they argue that private firms reduce costs by cutting quality—but it is not because of market forces; it is because the incorruptible market regulator called competition has been terminated and replaced with regulation by a corrupt (or perhaps simply inefficient) public official.

Of course, firms do not have to resort to illegal means in order to "purchase" contracts. The Florestano-Gordon survey (1980, 32) found that important "criteria" in awarding large contracts are "political considerations."

> In the political community, contractors are expected to make political contributions in order to be eligible for contracts. Contributions may take the form of outright bribes and graft but...the more popular form is the campaign contribution—outright grants, subscriptions to fund-raising dinners, and so on. Such potlatch may be expected to take its toll by raising the costs of contract services and loosening the assiduousness of inspection. (Fitch 1974, 513)

If corruption, politics, and the bureaucratic tendencies toward overregulation do not eventually undermine competition and destroy the potential for cost savings and quality enhancement, and if the resulting gains are not misdirected (e.g., more drug law enforcement rather than focusing on property and violent crime), then the criminal justice system might be improved through greater contracting. More complete voluntarily demanded privatization can avoid many of the pitfalls of contracting out, however, and generate more certain benefits. Citizens are already undertaking such voluntary privatization on a large scale, as explained in the section on "private protection." To see why, first consider the reasons for the low level of vital private inputs to public policing and prosecution.

PRIVATE INPUTS TO "PUBLIC" ARREST AND PROSECUTION

A huge portion of all crimes that come to the attention of police are those reported by victims. Furthermore, without victim and/or witness testimony, a very substantial portion of the criminals that are arrested could never be successfully prosecuted. But according to the Bureau of Justice Statistics' most recent victimization survey (BJS 1993), only about 39 percent of all Index I crimes (murder and manslaughter, sexual offenses, aggravated assault, robbery, burglary, larceny, and auto theft) are reported. The evidence on deterrence suggests that the "certainty" of punishment is a much more significant deterrent than the severity of punishment.[3] Thus, a major impediment to the criminal justice system's ability to deter criminals occurs at this first step of essential involvement by private citizens.

Why Don't More Victims Report Crimes?

Victims of crimes weigh the expected costs and benefits of reporting crimes before doing so. Victims' costs arising from reporting crimes and cooperating in prosecution can include (1) out-of-pocket expenses such as transportation, baby-sitting, and parking; (2) lost wages in order to meet with police and prosecutors and appear in court; (3) emotional and psychological costs brought on by rounds of questioning, confronting an assailant, and enduring a defense attorney's questions; and conceivably (4) retaliation by an offender who is either unsuccessfully prosecuted or not confined for very long.

Many of these costs are created by the rest of the criminal justice system. For instance, victims can lose wages as they endure seemingly endless delays and continuances due to the huge caseloads facing prosecutors and courts. Further, prosecutors often "use an assembly line organization for their work.... [D]ifferent prosecutors are stationed along the various stages of the process and handle all the cases that reach the processing stage....[T]his means that the victim, who may have already explained his case to several different police officers, now has to retell it to each new prosecutor" (McDonald 1977, 301).

Victimization surveys indicate that revenge and incapacitation (punishment and prevention of further crimes by the offender) are the two most important reasons for reporting violent crimes (BJS 1993, 34). For property crimes, a desire to recover the property (or to collect insurance) is also important.

---

3. For references to the literature, see Benson 1990: 253–56; or Rasmussen and Benson 1994a: 41–43.

But expectations of such benefits are small due to the low probabilities of arrest, prosecution, conviction, and punishment, and many victims know it. Consider these probabilities:

Probability of Arrest

The BJS report on crime victimization (1993, 33) found that approximately 11 percent of unreported robberies, 11 percent of unreported personal larcenies, 12 percent of unreported household larcenies, and 10 percent of unreported auto thefts were not reported because the victims believed that the police would "not want to be bothered." Similarly, 13 percent of unreported rapes were not reported because of a belief that the police are "inefficient, ineffective or biased."[4] These beliefs are justified. In 1992, for instance, only 39.0 percent of Kansas's reported violent crimes and 14.3 percent of its reported property crimes were cleared by arrest.

Probability of Prosecution

Even with an arrest, there is a high probability that the charges will be dropped. How many cases are dismissed at this stage is generally not known, and probably depends on the jurisdiction. For instance, over 84 percent of New York felony arrests in 1979 (88,095 out of 104,413) were dismissed (Neely 1982, 16). In explaining dismissals, prosecutors pointed to a lack of staff and to police failure to properly secure evidence (e.g., because of carelessness, overwork, or violations of the rights of the accused). Many more cases are dismissed because prosecutors believe convictions will be difficult to obtain. In this regard, if the victim appears unconvincing or unsympathetic, has "done something stupid" and appears to "deserve" what he or she got, or has a criminal record, the prosecutor is likely to dismiss the case (or plea bargain generously).

Another factor is that the arrested offender may flee before prosecution occurs. In 1971, for example, almost one-third of New York City's criminal defendants simply disappeared (Landes 1974, 289). Many alleged criminals must be released from jail

---

4. Fear of reprisal is another factor, but this also reflects victims' perceptions that the criminal justice system probably will not lock up and hold criminals (Wilson 1977: xv–xvi).

prior to trial, of course, due to court delay, limited jail space, and constitutional guarantees of bail. Two primary mechanisms exist for initiating release and ensuring appearance for trial.

Historically, defendants for most crimes have been freed from jail by guaranteeing appearance with the posting of a monetary bond. Most do not have enough money to post the bonds required for their crimes, however, so a private market has developed in which a commercial bail bondsman posts the entire bond in exchange for a fee. Bondsmen lose the bonds if defendants fail to appear in court, so they spend a good deal of time, effort, and money to guarantee appearance. If a defendant flees, a national network of private "bounty hunters" is notified. Bounty hunters' incentives to find fugitives are very strong since they do not get paid unless the fugitives are returned to court.

A "public bail" alternative developed in the mid-1960s with a stated goal of helping those accused of nonviolent crimes who could not afford to post a bond. However, "it rapidly evolved into an indiscriminate release mechanism to cap the jail population. It has failed miserably to accomplish any of its aims" (Reynolds 1994, 18). The system is administered by tax-funded pretrial release (PTR) bureaucracies. Its costs are high. For instance, the Harris County, Texas, PTR program, which cost an average of $356 per defendant in 1992, had one staff employee for every 16 defendants being supervised, compared to one staff person for every 87 defendants supervised by one of the county's private bail-bonding companies (Reynolds 1994, 19). Alleged offenders are interviewed by PTR staff, and recommendations are made to judges. Those released are freed under a "personal recognizance bond" (Monks 1986, 8). Essentially, the alleged offender promises the judge that he or she will appear in court when called.[5] Failure to appear presumably means that a specified fine or forfeiture can be collected, but since nothing is paid up front, these "bonds" provide very little in the way of real incentives to appear (Reynolds 1994, 18).

This type of "public bail" is now very widespread, and accused criminals obviously prefer it. PTR programs tend to

---

5. In some cases, a limited deposit bail may actually be required, wherein a defendant will be required to put up 10 percent of the specified fine or forfeiture.

release the prisoners who are most likely to appear, leaving the remainder for private bail bondsmen (BJS 1990; Sorin 1986), yet about 27 percent of defendants supervised by PTR agencies initially do not appear in court, compared to about 14 percent of those under a private bonding arrangement (Reynolds 1994; BJS 1990; Sorin 1986). Furthermore, private bail bondsmen have a fugitive rate after three years that may be less than 1 percent, compared to 8 percent for the public alternative (Reynolds 1994, 17).[6] Thus, many urban counties have more than 50,000 fugitives from PTR, and nationally the number probably exceeds a million (Reynolds 1994, 19). As public PTR has been implemented, the probability of prosecution has fallen.

Probability of Conviction

The probability of conviction given prosecution tends to be quite high, suggesting that this is one area of the criminal justice system that may be working well. Offsetting this impression is the fact that prosecutors probably have a good idea of the chances of conviction before they actually file accusations. Indeed, about 90 percent of all convictions in the United States are obtained by plea or charge bargaining. Criminals gain a reduced expected punishment from the bargain as many are convicted for lesser crimes and/or fewer crimes than were actually committed, prosecutors gain in that their conviction statistics increase and their workload decreases, and judges benefit as cases are cleared and pressure on the court docket is relieved (Schulhofer 1988).[7] Notice that the potential benefits for victims, revenge and incapacitation of the criminals, are both reduced.

---

6. Fugitive rates may vary from year to year, so they depend on the time period examined. Reynolds (1994: 17) reports rates of 3 percent for private bondsmen and 9.5 percent for public pretrial release after one year.

7. How much prosecutors bargain away in their plea bargaining probably depends on the jurisdiction, but a New York study found that most people arrested were *not* prosecuted and convicted for the crimes actually committed. In 1979, of the 16,318 New York felony arrests that led to indictments, 56 percent resulted in guilty pleas to lesser felonies, 16 percent ended with misdemeanor guilty pleas, 12 percent were dismissed after indictment, 3 percent resulted in some "other" disposition, and 13 percent went to trial. Significantly, the largest number of sentences that did not involve a prison term arose due to prosecutors' willingness to permit felons to plead guilty to lesser charges (Neely 1982: 16).

Probability of Punishment

Most offenders actually prosecuted and sentenced will not go to prison (the majority are sentenced to probation). For instance, a very rough estimate of the cumulative probability of imprisonment for reported crimes can be determined for Kansas using 1992 data: 2,802 prison admissions divided by 133,237 reported crimes = 2.1 percent. Many criminals admitted to prison are non-Index I felons (e.g., drug felons), however, who may not have committed any violent or property offenses at all (Rasmussen and Benson 1994a, 39–66), so this 2.1 percent exaggerates the portion of reported crimes resulting in imprisonment. And even if imprisoned, felons will probably serve only short sentences before being released. In Kansas, for instance, the average time served has dropped every year since 1989 when it was at 28.3 months, reaching 19.1 months in 1993. Thus, any hope that cooperating with police and prosecutors will protect the victim or others from the same criminal is almost always false. After all, roughly 70 percent of the offenders released from prison are rearrested.[8]

Conclusions

Not reporting is a natural reaction to the high cost of victim involvement with the criminal justice system relative to the low expected benefits due to the system's ineffectiveness, a reaction that has been common since the inception of criminal law (Benson 1990, 62–63; 1994a; 1994b). Thus, the recommendations made in the final section will focus on ways that each of the steps in the criminal justice process, from reporting to arrest to prosecution to conviction to punishment, can be improved through greater private-sector involvement.

---

8. For instance, a Rand Corporation study reported that 76 percent, 60 percent, and 53 percent of released felons in California, Texas, and Michigan, respectively, had been rearrested within three years of their release (Klein and Caggiano 1986). A study for the BJS using a sample of young parolees from 22 states found that 69 percent had been rearrested within six years of release from prison (Beck 1987). The rearrest rate also varies by characteristics of the criminals. In the BJS study, 90 percent of those with a history of six or more arrests were rearrested again, 59 percent of first-time offenders were rearrested, and 79 percent of those charged as adults before the age of 17 were rearrested during the next six years.

Indeed, in this context, there is another potential benefit from reporting that must be noted. Insurance companies require that crimes be reported before they will pay claims. Thus, 9 to 12 percent of the victims of theft, including motor vehicle theft, cite collection of insurance as a primary motivation for reporting (BJS 1993, 34). In other words, these crimes are reported not because victims expect the criminal justice system to produce benefits, but because the victims have invested in a form of private "protection" of their wealth: insurance.

Private citizens are also employing even more direct private means of protecting persons and property. Indeed, as Sherman (1983, 145–49) observed, "Few developments are more indicative of public concern about crime—and declining faith in the ability of public institutions to cope with it—than the burgeoning growth in private policing....Rather than approving funds for more police, the voters have turned to volunteer and paid private watchers."

THE NATURE AND GROWTH OF PRIVATE PROTECTION

"Watching" refers to observing people and places that criminals may attack and apprehending criminals in the act; "walling" describes actions designed to prevent criminal access to persons or property; and "wariness" characterizes adjustments in behavior to avoid crime (Sherman 1983). While private-sector involvement in all of these activities is clearly quite substantial, much of this involvement is undocumented. There are, nonetheless, a few surveys and studies that shed some light on the level of privatization. Although some are dated, indications of the types of privatization in protection and of trends in such privatization can be gleaned by comparing their findings.

Individuals

The Research and Forecasts (1983, 68) study of fear of crime asked survey respondents what protective measures they take in their homes and when they go out: "The answers revealed an extremely cautious and security-minded America." For instance, 56 percent said they kept their car doors locked most of the time while driving, 70 percent did so more often than not, and 44 percent indicated that they often planned their travel routes to avoid potentially dangerous places. When going out at night, 25 percent of the sample frequently had a whistle or weapon or were accompanied by a dog. Fifty-four percent of the women made certain they had a companion for night trips.

Almost everyone interviewed for Research and Forecasts (1983, 73) locked their doors when leaving and made people identify themselves before opening their doors. Fifty-two percent had added extra locks to their doors, 82 percent had someone watch their homes when they were away for a weekend, and 70 percent had newspaper and mail delivery stopped. Approximately one-fourth of the survey sample had automatic timers to switch lights on and off, and many had more sophisticated devices to turn televisions or stereos on and off. Fifteen percent of the respondents had burglar alarms, 8 percent had barred windows, and 52 percent indicated that they owned a gun to protect their homes. And people use their guns for protection. California had 126 justifiable homicides by private citizens in 1981, for instance, compared to 68 by police (California Department of Justice 1981).

Corporate Security

The Research and Forecasts report also surveyed "Fortune 1000" businesses. Most corporate headquarters had a "vast array" of security procedures and devices: 88 percent had building security checks; 66 percent had burglar alarms; 64 percent had floodlighting; 50 percent had automatic light timers; 48 percent had closed-circuit television; 38 percent had electronic card identification systems; 30 percent had photoelectric timers; and 24 percent had armed guards (Research and Forecasts 1983, 110). Four hundred of the companies used at least six of these eight security systems, and unarmed guards, plainclothes security personnel, and coded door locks were common. Most of the corporations also had comprehensive security programs, including employee education (73 percent), crisis management plans (63 percent), and employment of a security specialist (62 percent).[9]

---

9. Corporate executives also took numerous measures to protect themselves and their families: 75 percent of the senior executives surveyed secured their

Voluntary Group Actions Against Crime

A Gallup poll discussed by Sherman (1983, 145) indicated that organized volunteer crime prevention efforts were in place in the neighborhoods of 17 percent of the Americans surveyed. Podolefsky and Dubow's (1981, 44) random-digit telephone survey of San Francisco, Chicago, and Philadelphia suggested that "[m]ost of the activities reported as 'doing something about crime' involve attempts by groups of neighbors to improve the 'quality of life' in their neighborhood."

Programs for Youth

Youth-oriented activities accounted for the largest proportion (19.9 percent) of neighborhood crime control activities discovered by Podolefsky and Dubow (1981, 45). Some see youth programs designed to keep children busy, particularly sports programs, as major contributions to crime control, but many groups indicated that "recreation is not enough; there is a need to combine education, economics and recreation" (Podolefsky and Dubow 1981, 48). Thus, community groups frequently provide youth-oriented job counseling for employment opportunities.

Neighborhood Improvement

Improving or cleaning up the neighborhood was the third most frequently mentioned crime control activity in the Podolefsky-Dubow (1981, 53–54) survey, accounting for 8 percent of the responses. These included programs to (1) improve the physical and social conditions of their neighborhoods or communities, (2) alter conditions seen as particularly conducive to crime, (3) reduce access, (4) make changes that facilitate group watching (e.g., pruning trees and shrubs and installing lighting), and (5) improve the overall economic conditions of the area.

Property Protection

Community groups promote awareness and home security by

---

homes with burglar and fire alarms, had guards and guard dogs, had unlisted phone numbers, or kept their addresses confidential; 35 percent varied routes to work; and 19 percent alternated cars (Research and Forecasts 1983: 109).

holding meetings, arranging lectures, and distributing crime prevention literature (Podolefsky and Dubow 1981, 71). Some groups organize property-engraving programs. Participants are also urged to display decals that announce to potential burglars that they have marked their property (Skogan and Maxfield 1979). Participation in such programs ranged from 10 to 25 percent in target areas, and 31 percent of those surveyed by Podolefsky and Dubow (1981, 73) reported marking property.

Personal Protection

Group escort services are typically designed for a particular purpose, such as escorting senior citizens when they cash pension, social security, or welfare checks; accompanying children home from day-care centers; or escorting women students who must cross a campus after dark. Many people participated in organized response programs such as WhistleSTOP, in which participants carry a whistle that they can blow if they encounter trouble in the streets. Other WhistleSTOP members respond to a signal by first calling the police and then blowing their own whistles to signal others that a crime situation exists.

Surveillance Patrols

In 1977, between 800 and 900 resident patrols operated in urban areas with over 250,000 people, and there were more than 50,000 block watches nationwide. An estimated 63 percent of the patrols were composed of volunteers, 18 percent of hired guards, and 7 percent of paid residents; the remaining 12 percent involved a combination of voluntary and hired watchers. An estimated 55 percent of all patrols were found in low-income areas, 35 percent in middle-income areas, and 10 percent in high-income neighborhoods (Yin et al. 1977, 13).[10]

---

10. Corroborating evidence comes from New York, where in 1980, roughly 10,000 of the city's 39,000 blocks had functioning block associations to compensate for inadequate city services, and nearly all of these associations had some kind of security patrol. A "typical" voluntary patrol might be the East Midwood Patrol in Brooklyn. In 1980, the patrol had 120 volunteer members, who performed all-night patrols 365 days per year. They taught security techniques to households and watched for prowlers and muggers. Expenses were covered by $10/year donations from the houses in the 25-block patrol area; 85 percent of the households contributed in 1980 (Poole 1980: 38).

Building patrols typically operate in areas that receive little attention from public police, primarily in order to deter crime and keep undesirable strangers out of the building. Unlike building patrols, neighborhood patrols have frequent contact with public police and coordinate their efforts with police. Neighborhood patrols may operate on foot or in cars, and some observe crime-prone areas from fixed vantage points. They often use radios to report to a base station or to the police.[11]

Private Streets

One of the most complete cooperative privatization schemes in recent history occurred in St. Louis and University City, Missouri. As Oscar Newman (1980, 124) noted,

> buried within those very areas of St. Louis which have been experiencing the most radical turnover of population are a series of streets where residents have adopted a program to stabilize their communities, to deter crime, and to guarantee the necessities of a middle-class life-style. These residents have been able to create and maintain for themselves what their city was no longer able to provide: low crime rates, stable property values and a sense of community....The distinguishing characteristic of these *streets* is that they have been deeded back from the city...and are now legally *owned*...by the residents themselves. (Emphasis added)

In 1970, for example, Westminster Place in St. Louis was dying economically. An estimated 6,000 cars per day used Westminster Place to avoid traffic lights on nearby major boulevards, and prostitutes found the neighborhood to be an attractive business area. But in 1970, "standing up to the urban

---

11. Many neighborhood patrols are organized with the help of public police. Others have developed because of a perceived lack of public police presence (Marx and Archer 1971). For instance, the West Park Community Protection Agency was organized by a black resident of Philadelphia because "when Blacks began moving into the area police became lax" (Podolefsky and Dubow 1981: 81). The organizer performed stakeouts and patrols, checked in with businesses, and signed in on police sign-in sheets. The police initially accused him of vigilantism, but eventually recognized the benefits of cooperating with the group, and after a change in the organization's name, links with police were established. But this kind of cooperation does not always develop (Wooldridge 1970: 115).

blight, the crime, and the fear that causes residents to flee, the people of [Westminster Place and several other] neighborhoods...found an unconventional solution to a common problem": they petitioned the city to deed the streets to them (Gage 1981, 18). The city complied, in return for the residents' assumption of responsibility for street, sewer, and streetlight maintenance; garbage pickup; and any security services above normal fire and police protection.

The titles to the streets are now vested in incorporated street associations to which all property owners must belong and pay dues. The street associations, most of which own one or two blocks, have the right to close the street to traffic, so the only cars on the street belong to residents and their visitors. "It is *their* street and that ownership gives the neighborhood a high degree of cohesiveness" (Gage 1981, 19). As a result of cooperative behavior, private streets have significantly lower crime in virtually every category than comparable public streets (Newman 1980, 137, 140): Westminister Place's crime rate was 108 percent lower than the adjacent public street, for instance.

Many new residential developments involve private streets and some sort of private security arrangements from their inception. Entire developments are walled, with security guards posted at the gates. Similarly, large shopping centers have their own security forces and traffic enforcement. Thus, private streets are really not very unusual; what is unusual about the St. Louis experience is the deeding of formerly public streets to private citizens.

The Market for Security

Table 1 indicates that from 1964 to 1991, employment by private firms specializing in protective and detective services increased by 746.8 percent, and the number of firms offering such services grew by 543 percent.

The figures in Table 1 do not include direct employment of security personnel by firms, residential developments, and other institutions. A 1970 estimate put the number of privately employed "police," including internal security, at roughly equal to public police, but by 1983, there were over twice as many private security personnel as public police in the United States (Reichman 1987, 247). In 1991, a National Institute of Justice

Table 1. Number of Firms and Employees in SIC 7393: Detective Agency and Protective Services, 1964–1991

Year	Number of Firms	Number of Employees
1964	1,988	62,170
1967	3,389	151,637
1973	4,182	202,561
1976	5,841	248,050
1979	6,502	310,333
1982	8,424	345,874
1985	10,066	410,625
1988	11,675	473,308
1991	12,783	526,435
% change 1964–91	543.0%	746.8%
Average % change 1964–91	20.1%	27.7%

Source: Bureau of the Census, County Business Patterns (Washington, D.C.: U.S. Department of Commerce, Bureau of the Census, various years).
Note: *SIC 7393 was split into 7381 and 7382 in 1988.*

report estimated that the ratio had reached about 2.5 private security employees to each public police officer (Cunningham et al. 1991). Roughly $21.7 billion was paid to 1.1 million full-time security employees in 1980 (Cunningham and Taylor 1985, 12), and by 1991, these estimates had reached $52 billion for 1.5 million private security personnel (Cunningham et al. 1991).[12]

---

12. Even these employment estimates "greatly underestimate the extent of private policing. Surveillance of private places and transactions is being conducted by actors who traditionally have not been counted as among the rank and file of private police" (Reichman 1987: 246), such as insurance adjusters, corporate risk managers, and other "loss consultants."

Crime Deterrence Equipment

A 1970 study by Predicasts, Inc., estimated that sales of crime deterrence equipment grew at an annual rate of 8.8 percent from 1958 to 1963 and 11 percent from 1963 to 1968. Sales of monitoring and detection equipment grew by 7.1 percent per year over the 1958–1963 period and 10.4 percent per year from 1963 to 1968. Including spending for guard and investigative services, these equipment sales accounted for less than half the total expenditures on security during this period (41 percent in 1958 and 36 percent in 1968), and this relative level of expenditures apparently has continued to hold (Cunningham and Taylor 1985, 24). Nonetheless, "alarm systems are the most frequently used component of security programs," at least for businesses, and the residential market for such services is growing rapidly (Cunningham and Taylor 1985, 21). An estimated 10 percent of the homes in the United States were connected to central alarm systems in 1990, up from 1 percent in 1970 (Reynolds 1994, 8). Central stations for alarms are now provided by several national companies (e.g., Honeywell, Wells Fargo, Sonitrol, and Westinghouse) as well as by large numbers of small local firms (Cunningham and Taylor 1985, 21).[13]

Conclusions

Dissatisfaction with the performance of the government's criminal justice system means that victims are choosing not to report crimes, and that potential victims are turning to private alternatives for protection. It should not be surprising to find that victims are also turning to private alternatives to resolve crimes and sanction criminals.

PRIVATE JUSTICE

Private justice, "the localized nonstate systems of administering and sanctioning individuals accused of rule breaking or disputing within groups or organizations" (Henry 1987, 45-46), has a long

---

13. There is also a growing market for more "exotic" equipment like bullet-proof cars and vehicle security systems for those facing assassination or kidnapping risks (Dobson and Payne 1983).

and frequently misunderstood history. "Vigilante" actions, for instance, are an American tradition, but in contrast to its widespread characterization as "lynch-mob rule," vigilante movements almost always involved law-abiding citizens enforcing the law and *reestablishing order* following breakdowns in the government's legal system due to corruption and/or ineffectiveness (Valentine 1956; Stewart 1964; McGrath 1984; Benson 1990, 312–23). A similar breakdown is increasingly apparent today, both in criminal and in civil law. Briefly consider the shift of dispute resolution, for instance, into private forums.

Private Courts for Civil Justice: Implications for Criminal Justice

Commercial arbitration began in the American colonies and has almost continually grown in importance since then (Benson 1995). By the 1950s, at least 75 percent of all disputes between businesses were being settled through private arbitration (Auerbach 1983, 113). Most trade associations and commercial groups have developed their own arbitration arrangements, and others, such as the American Arbitration Association (AAA), offer private dispute resolution to businesses that do not belong to such groups (Benson 1994b). In fact, commercial arbitration has made "the courts a secondary recourse in many areas and completely superfluous in others" (Wooldridge 1970, 101).

Labor arbitration also has a long and well-documented history, but consumer arbitration may be less well known despite considerable history of its own. For instance, the New York Stock Exchange formally provided for arbitration in its 1817 constitution, and it "has been working successfully ever since," primarily to rectify disputes between exchange members and their customers (Lazarus et al. 1965, 27). Today, the Council of Better Business Bureaus has arbitration programs for consumers in many parts of the country, and it also arbitrates car owners' complaints for several automobile manufacturers; similarly, insurance companies arbitrate large numbers of claims, and medical malpractice arbitration is on the rise (Denenberg and Denenberg 1981, 6–10). Many other examples could be cited.

A Market for Justice

In 1976, California had a 70,000-case public court backlog, with a median pretrial delay of 50 and one-half months (Poole

1980, 2). Two lawyers who wanted a complex case settled quickly found a retired judge with expertise in the area of the dispute, paid him at attorney's-fee rates to resolve it, and saved their clients a tremendous amount of time and expense (Granelli 1981, 1-2). Following this, a new market for dispute resolution opened up. There is no count of these so-called "rent-a-judge" cases tried since 1976, but the civil court coordinator of the Los Angeles County Superior Court estimated that several hundred disputes had been so settled during the first five years. Most cases involve complex disputes that litigants "feel the public courts cannot quickly and adequately" try (Pruitt 1982, 51).

Private for-profit firms began organizing and entering the justice market in the late 1970s and early 1980s, and they now offer services in virtually every state. Judicial Arbitration and Mediation Services Company (JAMS), started in 1979 by a California state trial judge, has become the largest firm in the industry, with gross revenue growth of 826 percent from 1988 to 1992, in reflection of the "demand for relief from the jammed dockets and killer jury awards of the courts" (Phalon 1992, 126). Another for-profit dispute resolution firm, EnDispute, Inc., opened in Washington, D.C., and Los Angeles in 1982. The firm's revenues grew by 130 percent from 1988 to 1992 as it became the second largest in the industry, adding offices in Chicago, Cambridge, Massachusetts, and Santa Ana, California, and it is continuing to expand into other large markets.

JAMS and EnDispute recently attracted large investments by venture capitalists ($17 million was paid for a 60-percent share of JAMS, and $3 million was invested in EnDispute), not as start-up money, but as "late-stage expansion investments that have enabled JAMS and EnDispute to push their hearing rooms into big-city markets (New York, for one) that should add significantly to revenues" (Phalon 1992, 126). Judicate opened in Philadelphia in 1983, went public in 1985 with sales of stocks, and in March 1987 was employing 308 judges in 45 states. It has been called the "national private court" although it is actually only the third largest of the private court firms.[14] Several other firms are also

_____

14. Unlike some of its competitors (e.g., JAMS and EnDispute), Judicate has been facing financial difficulties, but in any free market, some firms will fail as others prosper.

active in this market (Benson 1990, 223–24), and they have moved from business disputes into personal injuries, divorces, warranty disputes, loan defaults, and so on.

Private Courts and Criminal Justice

Why discuss private courts for civil disputes in the context of an exploration of privatization in criminal law? Because, as Denenberg and Denenberg (1981, 26) point out, private "dispute resolution is a method whose potential applications are limited only by the ingenuity of the potential users." For instance, one of the earliest community dispute resolution projects, run by the American Arbitration Association in Philadelphia, began hearing minor criminal cases in 1969. During the 1970s and early 1980s, the AAA became increasingly involved in minor criminal and civil disputes, such as neighborhood fights and juvenile offenses (Poole 1978, 55). The success of this program provided the impetus for moving minor criminal cases into neighborhood justice centers. Similar arrangements followed the AAA's example.[15] Other private justice options are developing.

Informal Justice

Even when neighborhood dispute resolution arrangements are not formally developed by third parties (e.g., the AAA) and recognized by the government, they often exist. Informal private justice may be substantially less costly than formal alternatives, after all, and the benefits may be much more certain. Ellickson (1991, 213–14) described a typical process: (1) the offender is informed by the victim of an "informal debt" so that it can be resolved voluntarily by a "side-payment"; (2) if the debt is not paid, "truthful negative gossip" is spread about the unpaid debt; (3) once the neighbors have been informed of the offense and refusal to pay the debt, some appropriate amount of the offender's assets are either seized or destroyed.

---

15. It should be noted that some of these arrangements have involved substantial government roles in their development, financing, and administration. If the programs fail when funding is withdrawn, as has happened over the past few years, some observers may conclude that the private sector is unable to provide neighborhood- or community-based conflict resolution services. However, in all likelihood, the failures reflect characteristics of those particular community-based systems that have been imposed by public officials (Benson 1990: 217).

If the government punishes or attempts to prevent such "restitutive punishment," or if the offender is not a resident of the neighborhood (so the threat of gossip is not viable), the victim may simply go to the final step in the sequence outlined by Ellickson. And if seizure of an asset is treated as theft by the government, destruction of an asset belonging to the offender (vandalism), which is likely to be easier to cover up than a seizure, becomes the likely punishment (Ellickson 1991, 217). If the offense is severe, physical punishment (assault) may also occur. Clearly, a considerable amount of "crime" by private citizens may be "undertaken to exercise social control" (Ellickson 1991, 213).

Informal or formal associations may also aid the victim in exacting punishment. Recognition of the fact that a group will take such actions is a deterrent, so under some circumstances at least, a group may intentionally develop a reputation for being willing to "take the law into their own hands." Indeed, increasing numbers of neighborhood groups are "sanctioning wrongdoers" (e.g., drug addicts, pushers, drunks, prostitutes, and troublesome families) because they reduce the quality of the neighborhood (Podolefsky and Dubow 1981, 64). This is a natural reaction to the criminal justice system's failure to provide adequate protection and/or punishment.

Criminal Justice Administered within Business Organizations

Fireman's Fund Insurance Company estimates that one-third of all business failures are caused by employee theft (Cunningham and Taylor 1985, 8). These are thefts that presumably are prosecutable, but in reality, police tend to give them little attention, and the public-sector criminal justice system tends to be "unsympathetic to business losses due to crime" (Cunningham and Taylor 1985, 11–12).[16] Thus, the crime investigated most frequently by security personnel in business organizations is employee theft, and the majority of security

---

16. In addition, "time theft" (e.g., conducting personal business on company time, abuse of sick leave, and shirking) was estimated to cost employers $120 billions in 1981, and such theft is "virtually impossible to prosecute" (Cunningham and Taylor 1985: 8).

managers for business firms report that these crimes (and most other crimes by employees) are either solved through their own investigations followed by direct contact with a public prosecutor, thus bypassing public police, *or,* "more often," totally resolved "within the organization,"—close to half of all employee thefts are resolved internally (Cunningham and Taylor 1985, 11).

Indeed, some observers believe that within business organizations, "private justice may exert far greater control on citizens than the criminal justice system itself" (Cunningham and Taylor 1985, 12). The process may be formal, involving internal disciplinary bodies, boards, or panels (Henry 1987, 46), or informal, with confrontations and "negotiation" between security personnel or managers and accused offenders. Resulting sanctions include dismissal, suspension without pay, transfer, job reassignment or redesign to eliminate some duties, denial of subsequent advancement, and restitution agreements.

BENEFITS AND POSSIBLE PITFALLS OF PRIVATIZATION IN CRIMINAL JUSTICE

The rapid growth of private-sector efforts to prevent crimes and to resolve them once they are committed reflects more than simply a negative response to certain aspects of public-sector failures. Benefits of private production can be substantial "Few would argue that *ceteris paribus,* if private security services were drastically reduced or eliminated, reported crime, fear of crime, and prices of retail merchandise would rise" (Kakalik and Wildhorn 1971, vii). Of course, the same statement could apply for public police, and there also may be undesirable consequences of privatization, as suggested by the discussion of some of the characteristics of informal justice (although they arise in large part because such "vigilante" actions are treated as illegal, so those taking them must attempt to avoid detection). As Tullock (1970, 127-128) explained: "In every case, the problem that we face when deciding whether some activity shall be market or government is...the maximization of the [net] benefit. Clearly, neither method is perfect, and clearly, we are choosing between two techniques that will produce less than if we lived in a perfect world." The question is: how can scarce resources be allocated most effectively, since there is no perfect option?

Evaluating Private Security

Unfortunately, unlike the public sector, with its penchant for keeping records that make research relatively easy, data on the effectiveness of investments in various private-sector crime prevention and protection activities is difficult to obtain, and as a result, the question has attracted relatively little attention from researchers. Donovan and Walsh (1986) performed what apparently is the only full-scale evaluation of a large private policing system: security for Starrett City, a 153-acre complex in a high-crime area of Brooklyn, with 56 residential buildings containing 5,881 apartment units and about 20,000 racially and ethnically diverse but largely middle—income residents. Starrett City also has eight parking garages and one outdoor parking lot, a shopping center with 25 businesses, a recreation complex, various open spaces and parks, and one elementary, one intermediate, and two nursery schools. Security is provided by a 54-person private police force.

Of residents surveyed, 88.8 percent felt safe within Starrett City (Donovan and Walsh 1986, 56), and this perception was clearly warranted. Table 2 lists reported crimes per 1,000 persons for Starrett City, the 75th precinct, where Starrett City is located, New York state, and the United States for 1984 and 1985. As Donovan and Walsh conclude, "Starrett City must be considered one of the safest communities in the United States" (36).

After all, Starrett City's low crime rates do not reflect nonreporting. Residents are much more likely to report crimes than others in the 75th precinct, as evidenced by the fact that they report many more incidents of criminal mischief, trespass, petit larceny, reckless behavior, and disorderly conduct than are reported to public police. This may reflect recognition of the fact that the public police and courts will do very little in response to such reports, but it also suggests that private security will respond. Furthermore, 77.5 percent of the residents said that they would report an assault to the Starrett City security force, while only 12.6 percent would call the New York City Police Department. Similarly, 34 of the 35 Starrett City retailers would call Starrett security if they had a problem (the manager of a 30-store chain, one of which is in Starrett City, would call city police; Donovan and Walsh 1986, 75).

Table 2. Reported Crimes per 1,000 Residents, 1984 and 1985

Crime	United States		New York State		75th Precinct		Starrett City	
	84	85	84	85	84	85	84	85
Murder/ Manslaughter	0.08	0.08	0.10	0.10	0.30	0.20	20.00	0.05
Rape	0.36	0.39	0.32	0.32	0.90	0.83	0.05	0.10
Robbery	2.05	2.14	5.07	4.56	16.00	15.51	3.60	2.57
Assault	2.90	3.20	3.66	3.86	6.10	6.88	1.90	1.05
Burglary	12.64	13.41	12.57	12.55	15.40	15.26	2.10	0.40
Larceny	27.91	30.49	27.55	28.41	12.10	11.64	2.90	1.30
Auto theft	4.37	7.27	6.51	5.90	10.10	9.51	1.80	1.10

Source: Donovan and Walsh (1986, 31)

Non-Starrett City residents also benefited from the Starrett City security force. During 1985, Starrett City security officers responded to 13,248 requests for services (only 8.35 percent were for crime reports; 4.36 percent were for disputes, and 87.28 were "service calls"). If the New York City Police Department had been responsible for these calls, the 75th precinct would have faced an 18 percent increase in calls, assuming that all of them would have been made (Donovan and Walsh 1986, 68-72), thereby drawing police away from other activities or requiring much larger police budgets. The greater propensity to report crimes in Starrett City suggests that only a portion of the calls would have been made to public police, but crime would have been much higher in the area without the private security, so potentially, calls could have increased.

Additional Evidence

Most studies of crime deterrence have examined the effects of public-sector efforts while ignoring private-sector deterrence. However, Timothy Hannan (1982, 91) found that the presence of guards in banks "significantly reduce[s] the risk of robbery. Accepting point estimates, the magnitude of this reduction is approximately one robbery attempt a year for those offices which would have otherwise suffered a positive number of robbery attempts." Charles Clotfelter (1977, 874) considered the impact of private and public security services on the manufacturing, wholesaling, finance, insurance, and real estate sectors; his empirical results "indicate that private protective firms are more effective than public police at protecting firms in these industries" (the same is true for railroads, as noted below). He also found that private protection is more effective and more readily responsive in areas experiencing rapid population growth.

Patrols and neighborhood watches also appear to be effective crime prevention alternatives (Yin et al. 1977, 30). In this regard, it has been argued that the lower crime rates on private streets in St. Louis discussed above result from limiting access, but closures of public streets have been tried elsewhere, and "to the disappointment of the project directors, police statistics did not show any dramatic drop in crime" (Gage 1981, 20). The reduced crime rates discussed above suggest that private streets create strong incentives to cooperate in crime control.

Individual self-protection efforts may also be quite effective. Because of the controversy surrounding firearms, gun ownership has attracted more study than other forms of protection. After reviewing evidence from several sources, Kleck and Bordua (1983) concluded that "it is a perfectly plausible hypothesis that private gun ownership currently exerts as much or more deterrent effect on criminals as do the activities of the criminal justice system....[T]here is the distinct possibility that although gun ownership among the crime-prone may tend to increase crime, gun ownership among the noncriminal majority may tend to depress crime rates below the levels they otherwise would achieve."

Prices as Sources of Information

The price system determines how resources are allocated in a private market, and these allocative decisions are typically based on better information for both demanders and suppliers than allocative decisions made in the public sector. After all, buyers in private markets consume the goods and services they purchase, so they *benefit directly* from any time, effort, or expense invested in gathering information.[17] Thus, if consumers are willing to pay a high price for a service, it implies that relatively informed consumers think the service is desirable relative to the alternatives available, and tells producers that it is desirable (profitable) to produce the service. The relative prices of different goods and services inform producers of relative consumer evaluations and act to coordinate the resource allocation decisions by influencing relative profits. Therefore, this transmission of information to producers allows them to specialize in order to more accurately (and profitably) meet the specific needs of individual consumers. Consider, for example, the railroad police, established at the end of World War I as complete and autonomous police forces.

Railroad police have compiled what must be considered a "remarkable" record of effectiveness, particularly relative to public police forces. Wooldridge (1970, 117) observed that the primary reason for this success is that the railroad police specialize in one area of enforcement, developing "an expertise not realistically within the grasp of public forces." Between the end of World War I and 1929, for instance, freight claim payments for robberies fell by 92.7 percent, from $12,726,947 to $704,262 (Wooldridge 1970, 116). This success has continued. In 1992, major railroads in the United States employed a 2,565-person security force which cleared about 30.9 percent of the crimes reported to them. Public police cleared about 21.4

---

17. Government producers (or even governments contracting out for services) do not persuade consumers to buy their individual services. Some consumers may be persuaded to support candidates offering a large bundle of services, but then taxes are collected and individual services are produced whether they are valued at their "tax prices" or not. Consumers of government services often do attempt to inform producers of what they want, of course, but the information transfer mechanism is very imperfect relative to price signals reflecting individual consumers' valuations of services. Furthermore, if individuals invest in gathering information in order to choose the candidate offering the best bundle of government policy, there is no guarantee that the candidate will be elected or that the policy will actually be provided if the candidate is elected. Thus, consumers of government services tend to be relatively uninformed about options, and less able to inform producers of their wishes (indeed, the vast majority clearly recognize this and do not even bother to vote), so government producers have a great deal of discretion in allocating resources. Rationing in the public-sector criminal justice system is obviously much more complicated than suggested here, of course: for details, see Benson 1990 or Rasmussen and Benson 1994a and 1994b.

percent of reported crimes, but because of their relative effectiveness, it is estimated that 75 percent of all crimes against railroads are reported to their police force, compared to 39 percent for public police. Therefore, adjusted for reporting, clearance rates were 8.1 for public police and 23.2 for railroad police (Reynolds 1994, 11–12). Furthermore, arrests by railroad police produced an overall conviction rate at close to 98 percent over the years (Dewhurst 1955, 4), roughly two to six times the conviction rates from public-police arrests, depending on the type of crime and the jurisdiction. This kind of specialization and consequent proficiency (and efficiency) often characterize private firms.

Potential Spillover Benefits of Privatization: Improved Public-Sector Performance

Kakalik and Wildhorn (1971, 117) pointed out that "private police often act as extended eyes and ears for the public police; they occasionally assist in serving warrants and citations on private property, or in traffic control around private property; they report suspicious persons and circumstances to public police; they may make preliminary investigations; they may make, or assist in making, arrests; they may apprise police of impending unusual situations, such as strikes; and so on." Similar results can arise with voluntary watches and patrols. When private activities cooperate with, or "complement," public police, public law enforcement becomes more effective. The most recent major study of private security sees privatization as a "substitution" of private for public security (Cunningham and Taylor 1985), however, rather than as complementary development (see also Clotfelter 1977 and Benson 1990, 249–51, 261–62). Nonetheless, the threat of loss of budgets and jobs may induce public criminal justice officials to develop stronger cost-monitoring and innovation incentives. Thus, both private substitutes and complements for public services can enhance the performance of the public sector.

Criticisms of Privatization in Criminal Justice: Are They Valid?

Critics of privatization in criminal justice contend that the emphasis on efficiency and effectiveness tends to overlook important flaws and failings. These criticisms are generally incorrect when applied to competitive markets, however (although they often may be correctly applied to government production or to a "market" controlled by corrupt or inefficient regulators).

"The Profit Motive Leads to Cost Cutting and Poor Quality."

Private police firms presumably will reduce quality and cut corners to raise profits, as evidenced by the "undertrained," "old," "high-school dropouts" that work as security personnel (*U.S. News and World Report* 1983). First, the evidence is false. Cunningham and Taylor's (1985, 89) survey found that the average age of private security personnel was between 31 and 35, and over half (59 percent) had at least some college education. Similarly, the average age of the Starrett City security force was 39, 83.3 percent of the officers had at least high school educations, 70.4 percent of them had prior security experience before taking the Starrett City job (over 25 percent had been either a public or a military police officer), and all of these security officers had received prior security training, either from another security agency or from the New York City Police Academy (Donovan and Walsh 1986, 37–42).

Second, the premise is false. The only circumstances under which the quality-cutting argument holds are when (1) sellers have only short-term profit goals, or (2) the market is not competitive. There are con men and hucksters in some markets who move into an area for a short period, defraud a number of consumers, and move on, of course; but no matter how uninformed consumers might be, it is unlikely that many of them would buy security services from such fly-by-night operations. A sense of permanence and a reputation for quality services would clearly be much more important criteria for consumers choosing such services than the quality-cutting argument assumes. That is why firms "invest" in building reputations by providing quality— such investments pay off in higher long-run profits.

The number of private protection and detective agencies in the United States probably exceeds 13,000 today, and competition is fierce. When competitive firms have long-range profit goals, their incentives are to beat the competition by offering the same quality of service at lower prices (and, therefore, lower costs) or superior quality at comparable prices (i.e., increased quality without increased costs). After all, profits are *total revenues minus total costs*, so when reducing costs and quality means losing customers and revenue, profits fall.

The fact is, of course, that it would be foolish to employ a person with the training of an urban police officer as a night watchman (e.g., to check ID cards and set off an alarm in the event of trouble), or to pay the $20,000 to $40,000 it would cost to hire that person. On the other hand, it would be foolish to hire someone to design and initiate a corporate security system who has only the training and skills of an urban police officer. The market does provide minimum-wage watchmen to those consumers who demand them, but "virtually ignored [by the critics of private security] are the many thousands of well-qualified proprietary loss control personnel" (Bottom and Kostanoski 1983, 31). In fact, increasing technological sophistication in electronic detection equipment plays an important role in the increased proficiency of and demand for private police, and this requires skilled personnel. Thus, "there is emerging a new security person, highly trained, more highly educated and better able to satisfy the growing intricacies of the security profession" (Ricks et al. 1981, 13).

Abuses of Power

Private security officers are sometimes characterized as "armed and dangerous"—disgruntled people who want to be police officers but cannot make the grade, and who frequently use too much force. Edward Iwata (1984, 10) implied as much when he reported that in 1983, 22 people in California were killed in shooting incidents involving private security personnel. Iwata failed to point out, however, that there are at least two to three times as many private police as public police in California and that public police kill many more people than private police do. In 1981, for instance, 68 "justifiable homicides" were committed by California public police (California Department of Justice 1981). This does not include police officers killed, as Iwata's figure for private police does.

The fact that private police commit relatively little violence is not very surprising, however, since less than 10 percent of the total private security force is armed (Cunningham and Taylor 1985, 20). Guardsmith, one of the largest national firms, for instance, estimated that only 3 percent of its uniformed personnel were armed in 1985. Security managers report that while customers increasingly request armed guards, these requests are discouraged, both because they feel that weapons are generally not needed and because they face more liability and higher insurance costs when employees are armed (Cunningham and Taylor 1985, 20).

Private police are also not disgruntled rejects from the public police. Cunningham and Taylor (1985, 38–39) reported, for example, that many senior public-sector law enforcement personnel are actually attracted into private security because most security directors and many security managers now earn more than they do. More significantly, their extensive survey "tends to confirm other research indicating that 1) private security personnel are drawn from different labor pools than law enforcement officers, and 2) their personal characteristics are consistent with the functions they perform" (1985, 67). In fact, Table 3 (from Donovan and Walsh 1986) shows that the Starrett City force was, in general, more satisfied with what they were doing than were New York City public police officers. Thus, while security companies actively "discourage employees from detentions, searches, and the use of force" (Cunningham and Taylor 1985, 34), they apparently go well beyond that by employing people who are inclined to be very "service oriented" relative to public police (Donovan and Walsh 1986, 49), as suggested in Table 4. And this pays off: for instance, the "concern shown by security personnel for care of property and prevention of disorder as well as the safety of residents and visitors" explains the high level of reporting in Starrett City (Donovan and Walsh 1986, 36).[18]

Kakalik and Wildhorn (1971) surveyed 17 state and 24 local licensing authorities to find out about complaints against security firms. Among the state agencies, five apparently did not believe the problem was sufficient to warrant compiling data, and Delaware, Iowa, and Minnesota collected data but had no complaints to report for 1970. Similarly, seven local agencies did not compile data, and three that did reported no complaints.

---

18. A notable example of nonabusive characteristics is the very large private security operation at Disney World, described in Shearing and Stenning 1987.

Overall, the average complaint rate was 6 percent of the private firms for state regulators and 4.3 percent for local regulators. This low level of complaints is not surprising. Private firms must satisfy customers to stay in business. A security officer who abuses shopping-mall patrons will not be an officer for long.

Table 3. Job Satisfaction: Private and Public Police

	Starrett City _Security Officers_	New York City _Police Officers_
Overall Job Satisfying	77.77%	75.71%
Job Interesting	98.15	82.14
Feeling of Helping People	81.48	79.14
Work Role Satisfying	93.60	88.06
Feeling of Accomplishment	94.12	64.18
See Results of Work	88.24	47.14

Source: Donovan and Walsh 1986, 47.

Table 4. Service Orientation: Private and Public Police

	Starrett City _Security Officers_	New York City _Police Officers_
Enjoy Assisting Citizens in Non-Crime Situations	94.34%	81.62%
Always Comply with Requests for Assistance	94.44	30.60
Enjoy Incidents that Require Investigation	84.91	92.14
Feel They Receive Adequate Support from Citizens	80.77	40.60
Feel Citizens Have Right to Complain about Improper Behavior by Officer	98.15	91.24
Feel that Citizens Respect Security Officers	81.48	49.64
Total % of Officers with Service Orientation	96.30	59.57

Source: Donovan and Walsh 1986, 49.

Actually, many individuals, whether publicly or privately employed, might abuse their positions by cutting costs, doing poor-quality work, and bullying *if they can*. The institutional arrangements within which people perform their tasks determine whether or not such abuses can be carried out, and competitive markets are one of the best (if not *the* best) institutional arrangements designed to discourage abusive, inefficient behavior. Beyond that, an individual who is not fully responsible for the consequences of his actions is likely to be *relatively* unconcerned about those consequences.

A civil suit brought against an abusive private security firm can be very costly, perhaps even destroying the business. In a suit against a public law enforcement agency, however, taxpayers pick up the tab, so the cost to the manager of that agency is relatively small. Furthermore, a public police officer cannot even be sued for false arrest unless the plaintiff can prove that he or she is innocent *and* that the police officer had no reason to suspect that individual. In addition, no legal claim against the government or its officials can be made by an innocent person who is wrongly imprisoned. It might be recognized that the government has made an error, but government officials have the *legal right* to make such errors and are not liable for them. Not surprisingly, tales of public police abusing suspects are quite common.

"Markets Favor the Rich"

Yet another argument against privatization is that only the wealthy can afford private security. Rich and poor certainly do not have access to precisely the same private security resources. Indeed, as Lott (1987) stressed, someone who earns a high wage should be able to employ security services because that person's own time has valuable alternative uses. Thus, an array of private participatory and hired security are available so individuals can choose according to their willingness and ability to pay, with either money or time.[19]

More fundamentally, the cost of the public-sector criminal

---

19. Historical evidence also suggests that private arrangements will be made to ensure that attacks against poor victims are brought to justice (Friedman 1979; Benson 1990).

justice system is disproportionately borne by the poor. The probability that a woman from a family making under $3,000 a year will be raped is almost four times that for a woman from a family that makes $25,000 or more; the same is true for other violent crimes (Neely 1982, 140). Furthermore, since such victims are also more likely to make less-than-articulate witnesses (or to have criminal records themselves), "it is more likely that these cases are given away by prosecutors than those of higher income victims" (McDonald 1977, 300). And as Neely (1982, 140) explained: "In terms of tax revenues, the release of dangerous felons is very cheap. The cost of the sanction is then shifted [to the poor] because that is the class that disproportionately bears the brunt of crime" (they pay taxes too, of course, at least through their rents and purchases). Thus, for the poor, privatization potentially means switching from a system to which they currently contribute but from which they feel alienated to a system where they get the protection and justice they pay for.

Conclusions

Market imperfections are not nearly as severe as many critics of private law enforcement have suggested. The evidence regarding government failures in criminal justice is overwhelmingly clear, however, as is suggested by its dismal performance in arresting, prosecuting, and punishing criminals.[20] Thus, a vital policy concern should be: how can we encourage greater private-sector involvement in criminal justice?

PRIVATIZATION IN CRIMINAL JUSTICE: POLICY ALTERNATIVES

The expected punishment for a person contemplating a crime is determined by the probabilities that (1) the crime will be reported, (2) the criminal will be arrested, (3) the criminal will be charged and prosecuted, (4) the prosecution will be successful

---

20. For discussion and rejection of other arguments against privatization, see Benson 1990: 271-328, and for analysis of the causes and consequences of government failure in criminal justice, see Benson 1990: 43-175 and Rasmussen and Benson 1994a.

and a sentence will be imposed, and (5) the criminal will serve the sentence actually imposed. The following discussion focuses on a wide range of policy changes that should encourage greater private-sector involvement in order to change these probabilities, thereby increasing deterrence and reducing crime.

Encouraging More Reporting

The probability of victim reporting can be increased by lowering the costs and/or raising the benefits of cooperating with arrests and prosecutions. The benefits of cooperation can be raised by increasing the probabilities of arrest, prosecution, conviction, and punishment, of course (issues discussed below), and the growing political importance of the victims' rights movement has produced a number of changes in many states that are intended to do so, primarily (although certainly not exclusively) by focusing on punishment and/or incapacitation. These include laws mandating tougher sentencing, the right of victims to testify or to file a written victim impact statement prior to sentencing, elimination of criminal defenses such as drugs or alcohol use or insanity as mitigating circumstances in violent acts, notification for victims before a criminal is paroled, and numerous other reforms.

Some local jurisdictions are also experimenting with various ways to reduce the cost of cooperation. In one New York jurisdiction, for instance, a single prosecutor now works with a victim of a sex crime for the entire prosecution process, thus becoming more personally involved with the victim and therefore more concerned about the victim's perspective on the process and its outcome. To the degree that such measures are successful, increased reporting should result.

Public compensation for victims has also been established in several states. There may be important reasons to support compensation programs, but the fact is that no compensation program can budget enough to cover the cost of crime for even the majority of victims.[21] A superior option is victim restitution.

---

21. There are actually a number of problems with the way compensation programs have been developed and implemented as well, which make it costly for victims to recover. See Meiners 1977 and Benson 1990, 153–154 for discussions.

Restitution

Many states now have laws that require judges to consider restitution in sentencing decisions, but restitution is generally viewed as an alternative *punishment* rather than a mechanism for restoring victims. Thus, for instance, state courts ordered only 16 percent of convicted felons to pay restitution in 1990 (Reynolds 1994, 29). But more significantly, the criminal justice system has been either inefficient or impotent at enforcing restitution orders even when they are made (Pudlow 1993, E1).

There is no hope of collecting restitution if a criminal goes to prison, given the political constraints on prison work programs discussed below, and when criminals are sentenced to probation, the supervising officers charged with collecting restitution are generally unable or unwilling to do so. Redirecting criminal justice by establishing a restitution-based rather than a punishment-based system would create stronger incentives for victims to report crimes and cooperate in prosecution, thus increasing the certainty of punishment and generating greater deterrence (as noted below, this redirection can be facilitated by privatizing the collection of restitution).

Increasing the Probability of Arrest

A 1990 survey of state and local police departments (Reaves 1992b, 4) reported that police are responsible for many activities that may not deter any crimes or produce any arrests: 96 percent of the surveyed departments performed accident investigation, over half operated the community's telephone and radio emergency communications and dispatch services (e.g., 911 services), 43 percent had animal control duties, 33 percent did search and rescue, 18 percent had emergency medical services, 18 percent provided court security, 14 percent did civil defense, 10 percent provided civil process serving, and so on. A similar survey found that sheriffs' departments are even more likely to perform non-law-enforcement functions (Reaves 1992a).

With so many duties, public police are unable to respond to many calls for assistance (e.g., see Table 4). Indeed, many police departments do not send an officer in response to calls regarding certain crimes, particularly larcenies and burglaries.

One way to increase the police's ability to make arrests and deter crimes is to contract out nonsecurity services, such as accident investigation, funeral escorts, animal control, emergency communications and dispatch services, search and rescue, emergency medical services, civil defense, and civil process serving, so that the police can specialize in crime-related activities.

Watching to Prevent versus Waiting to Arrest

The function of public police in the minds of most citizens is to "fight crime," but how can voters, taxpayers, and/or elected representatives tell if police are doing a good job? The number of arrests and "response times" after crimes are reported are the primary "statistics" that police focus on as "output" measures to justify budgets (Sherman 1983, 156). It is not surprising, therefore, that after an extensive review of research on police performance, Sherman (1983, 149) concluded: "Instead of *watching to prevent crime*, motorized police patrol [is] a process of merely *waiting to respond* to crime" in order to make arrests.

There is a growing body of evidence implying that taking police officers out of the "emergency response system"—so they can patrol neighborhoods on foot and actively watch—creates more effective crime prevention (Skolnick and Bayley 1988) and gives the officer better information about the problems and people of the neighborhood (Trojanowicz and Moore 1988). As Sherman (1983, 149) lamented: "In general, as the level of *crime prevention watching* has declined, the level of crime has risen."[22]

Payments to private security personnel and benefits for voluntary watchers arise from protection of persons and property, rather than from making arrests after crimes are committed. Thus, private security personnel provide the kind of policing services that "community policing" advocates say public police should be providing. This suggests that public police should not be the primary providers of crime prevention (see

---

22. There is considerable empirical support for the hypothesis that a higher probability of arrest deters crime; see Benson 1990: 254–56 for a review. The argument made here is not inconsistent with this empirical result, but rather, it suggests that waiting to arrest is *not the most effective* way to deter crime.

also Sherman 1983). In this vein, security services performed by police are often identified as candidates for contracting out, including public-building security, parking enforcement, patrolling public parks, special-event security, court security, prisoner transport, and patrolling public housing developments (Cunningham et al. 1991, 2), and it may be appropriate to go much further. For example, the northern section of San Francisco has 62 "private police beats" that are "owned" by private "patrol specialists" (Dorffi 1979). All have completed police academy training and have full rights to carry firearms and make arrests. However, they are paid by the businesses, home owners, and landlords on their "beats." Each patrol specialist purchases a beat from its previous owner and then negotiates contracts with each property owner on the beat who wishes to purchase his or her services. The level of attention required by a customer determines the fee. In order to encourage greater use of such privatization, however, elimination of various barriers to the effective use of private policing is required.

Lowering the Legal Barriers to Privatization in Policing

Statutes in many states mandate that private police and citizens in general cannot take people into custody, let alone gather evidence for trial or cite suspects in court. Some governments have granted private security personnel either full or limited police powers within confined areas, such as the San Francisco police beats. In New York, for instance, retail security personnel can act as agents of their employers and apprehend suspects, cite the suspects in court, and preserve evidence if they have completed an approved course of training. Some states grant similar powers in plants, stores, campuses, or retail malls, but this is limited. In a survey of private security managers, only 29 percent reported that they had some special police powers (Cunningham and Taylor 1985, 16). Private security should be able to obtain "police powers" under many more circumstances than is typically the case.

Licensing and regulatory restrictions may appear to be desirable mechanisms for protecting citizens from inferior services by unqualified personnel, but the reality is that licensing often creates a barrier to entry, preventing competition (Stigler 1971), and competition is often a much more effective regulator than government. Indeed, security managers, who by-and-large favor state licensing (probably in part because it provides a signal of reliability to uninformed consumers, but perhaps also because it can limit competitive entry to challenge established firms) recognize that licensing and regulatory boards dominated by industry representatives "lead to a limitation on competition, through the enactment of provisions that only certain firms could meet" (Cunningham and Taylor 1985, 28).

Private security firms are also increasingly being seen as a threat to police budgets and job security (Cunningham and Taylor 1985, 43). Nonetheless, of the 35 states that required guard and patrol firms to be licensed in 1985, 15 regulated through the State Police or Department of Public Safety (Cunningham and Taylor 1985, 28), while 7 regulated through a Department of Commerce or Occupational Licensing Agency and 5 did so through the Department of State. Not surprisingly, "[o]f these mechanisms, the regulation by law enforcement agencies appears to be the least popular....[S]ecurity firms generally oppose the practice....[It] has led to unfair and counterproductive controls, such as an overemphasis on police training in the curriculum for security guards" (Cunningham and Taylor 1985, 28-29). When police are in charge of regulating their competition, the predictable result is limits on competition through unnecessarily strict regulations and licensing requirements.[23] Thus, if regulation and licensing are desirable, they clearly should be done by some agency other than the police. Furthermore, as a National Institute of Justice study recommended, there should be "regulation and licensing reciprocity between states" in order to overcome the barriers to serving multistate clients, as well as other costs that arise because of varying requirements and limitations on powers across states (Cunningham et al. 1991, 4).

Local ordinances and licensing of security firms appear to be even more troubling than state regulations. For one thing, differing requirements across jurisdictions can create barriers to

---

23. More generally, employees, who may have the largest stake in government enforcement of crime, provide strong opposition to privatization. Public-police organizations successfully undermined the contracting out of police services in Arizona by threatening a lawsuit, for instance, as noted above. See Benson 1990: 332-38 and Wynne 1978: 198-228 for other examples.

successful security operations, raising the costs for firms serving regional clients, preventing the pursuit of suspects across jurisdictions, preventing testimony, and so forth. Also, these local regulations are even more likely to be in the control of or easily manipulated by police interests. About one-third of the law enforcement agencies surveyed by Cunningham and Taylor (1985) had the power to suspend or revoke private security licenses, for instance, and law enforcement executives strongly advocate even more widespread use of city and county ordinances granting them such powers. In contrast, the Cunningham et al. (1991, 4) report for the National Institute of Justice recommended that licensing and regulation should be "through state, not local" authorities. If licensing is to be done, this recommendation should be followed.

One reason for worrying about the quality of private security, and therefore one justification for regulation, is that security personnel may be criminals. However, this reflects the fact that security firms are generally denied access to criminal records of job applicants. Both the 1985 (Cunningham and Taylor 1985, 65) and 1991 (Cunningham et al. 1991, 4) National Institute of Justice reports recommend that all security employers have access to criminal records in order to screen their applicants. This would reduce the need for regulatory oversight, but more significantly, because the private firms are generally liable for the actions of their employees, they have stronger incentives to carefully screen applicants than public officials do (firms often obtain applicants' criminal records "illegally," so this would legalize what many firms feel compelled to do in order to provide quality services).

Private Streets

Watching activities by private citizens should also be encouraged. One way to do so is for public police to cooperate in the formation of "crime watch" programs. However, private streets create even stronger incentives for neighbors to cooperate in watching to prevent crime (Newman 1980; Gage 1981). Private streets are common in new residential developments, but the potential gains from privatization of streets should also be allowed in areas where public streets have been established.

Restitution and Private Pursuit of Criminals

Insurance companies investigate crimes under some circumstances (e.g., if their losses are large enough to warrant the cost of investigating). Many private organizations and businesses employ private investigators to do criminal investigations. The American Banking Association and the American Hotel-Motel Association both contract with the Wm. J. Burns International Detective Agency because they do not get satisfactory results from public police (Reynolds 1994, 12). However, by focusing on restitution for victims, the scope for private investigation and pursuit would expand considerably.

Victims could offer portions of their restitution as rewards. Specialized firms (bounty hunters) would arise to pursue criminals and collect fines. Alternatively, if the right to restitution were transferable (Friedman 1979), a victim might simply sell the right to collect a particular fine, or contracts with protection firms might include insurance payments to clients who are victimized and transfer of rights to collect restitution to firms that pursue offenders and recover insurance payments.

Contacting Out by Communities for Full Police Services

Contracting out for police services appears to be an effective way for a small community to lower costs while simultaneously increasing the quality of policing (Gage 1982; Benson 1990, 186). Whether this is true in general is a question that is unlikely to be "tested" in the current political environment, however, because many states have significant barriers to such contracting due to limits on "police powers," as noted above. Such barriers clearly should not apply to firms under contracts with government units.

Increasing the Probability of Prosecution

The growth in the use of public pretrial release (PTR) systems since the 1960s may help explain the much higher rates of crime that the country is now experiencing, both because the probability of fleeing from prosecution has risen and because serious crimes are being committed by individuals released on the recommendations of PTR agencies. Some state legislatures have passed Uniform Bail Acts in an effort to constrain the agencies' discretion (e.g., they may specify that no one can be released without a monetary bond who has a prior criminal record or who has "jumped" a previous free-recognizance bond), and more significantly, some judges are simply refusing to deal with PTR agencies (Reynolds 1994, 19). These judges are right: as Reynolds (1994, 19) concludes, taxpayer-funded PTR programs should be abolished so that the private bail-bonding system can take over full responsibility for supervision of accused criminals who are released pending prosecution.

There is a more fundamental problem with prosecution, however. Every accused criminal is guaranteed counsel, but while the public prosecutor supposedly represents victims, there are far too many crimes and victims for prosecutors to effectively represent. Thus, prosecutors must plea bargain away victims' charges or simply drop charges for many of the criminals that they face. Why not allow private prosecution? After all, history tells us that private prosecution can work. Indeed, it was the norm in England until this century (Cardenas 1986). Of course, an important question is: how would a private citizen finance the prosecution of a criminal? One possibility is a voucher system such as the one suggested by Schulhofer and Friedman (1993) for privatizing indigent defense and eliminating the public-defender bureaucracy (another attractive avenue for privatization).

Restitution and Private Prosecution

A superior solution to the question of how to pay for private prosecution (and one that simultaneously creates incentives to pursue prosecution) is the refocusing of the criminal justice system on restitution, including repayment for the costs of collection (e.g., prosecution and supervision of payment). Effectively, this turns crimes with victims into torts, giving victims strong incentives to pursue prosecution in order to collect damages (Benson 1990, 349–78). This is not a far-fetched idea. For instance, in France, a crime victim can file a civil claim against the accused, and this claim can be filed in a criminal court for consideration at the same time that the criminal case is being prosecuted. Furthermore, the civil suit can be filed in criminal court even before a public prosecutor files criminal proceedings.[24] As a result, "[p]rivate prosecution is very popular in France, since it enables the victim to collect damages quickly and inexpensively" (Cardenas 1986, 385).[25]

Increasing the Probability of Conviction

One major factor contributing to increases in crime is that courts apply very stringent standards for admitting evidence (National Advisory Commission on Criminal Justice Standards and Goals 1973, 206). These "exclusionary rules" shackle prosecutors' ability to bring the guilty to justice (Jones 1979, 83). And the fact is that civil liberties for the *innocent* have not been effectively protected by exclusionary rules. For instance, if the police enter a home, destroy or damage household property, and find nothing incriminating, exclusionary rules do not protect the home owner, whose only recourse is a damage suit, and such suits are frequently not successful. Public police's liability is limited by requiring proof of vicious intent or prior knowledge of innocence before damages will be paid (Neely 1982, 144-45). Thus, "there is little effective remedy against the police available to those who are not guilty," and "for every search that produces contraband there are untold scores that do not" (Barnett 1984, 54).

---

24. Courts are already overwhelmed with tort litigation, of course, but generally in areas of rapidly changing law (Benson forthcoming; Hensler et al. 1987). Once restitution law was clarified, this problem would become somewhat less significant. Furthermore, if a judge in France finds a claim to be groundless, the accuser pays the court costs and damages to the accused, and if the accusation is believed to be intentionally false, criminal charges can be brought against the accuser (Cardenas 1986: 386); that should be done in the United States for criminal law (and, indeed, for tort cases in general), even when a police officer is the accuser. Finally, if private courts are allowed to settle restitution disputes, as suggested below, the court crowding problem can be mitigated.

25. Other countries also allow some private prosecution. In England, some 3 percent of criminal prosecutions are done by victims (Cardenas 1986). Germany, like the U.S., has created a virtual public monopoly over prosecution, but they have two exceptions that do not exist in the U. S. (Reynolds 1994: 27). First, a class of misdemeanors, including things such as domestic trespass, can be prosecuted by victims. Second, a crime victim can demand that the public prosecutor pursue a case, and if the demand is refused, the victim can appeal to the court. If the court orders prosecution, the victim can act as a "supplementary prosecutor" to ensure that the public prosecutor adequately presents the case.

Privatization and Exclusionary Rules

Given their goals, the courts have little option but to establish exclusionary rules. Rules of evidence are under the court's control, but more efficient means of achieving the desired end are not. West Virginia Supreme Court Justice Neely (1982, 162) contends that if a state legislature were to enact a comprehensive compensation system for all citizens with reasonable money damages for *all* unconstitutional police intrusion and simultaneously prohibit the use of exclusionary rules in the state's courts, the Supreme Court would be forced to reconsider these rules.

Essentially, Neely has proposed that undermining the need for exclusionary rules requires that public police be privatized, at least to the degree that they face liability rules similar to those faced by private security firms. This would enhance the probability of conviction by removing protections that are intended to protect the innocent but end up protecting the guilty. Of course, one way to achieve this goal is to contract with private firms that are already liable for the misbehavior of employees. Indeed, as Cunningham and Taylor (1985, 12) noted, "cases brought by private security are usually well developed"—not surprising given their liability rules.

Restitution and Private Courts

Informally, sanctions are being imposed within business firms and by various other groups of private citizens, as noted above, thus reducing the demands on public courts and perhaps the need to dismiss and/or plea bargain so many cases. Civil liberty concerns about private judges mandating punishment will probably prevent the development of formal private-sector criminal courts, but formal private courts could move into criminal justice very quickly if the system were refocused on restitution, making the issue one of determining damage payments, at least for most crimes. Deciding damage awards is, after all, a frequent function of private courts.

Furthermore, as explained below, restitution decisions are actually likely to involve contracts specifying debts and how they should be paid—an issue regularly handled by private mediators and arbitrators. Thus, under a restitution system, the number of courts available would expand dramatically, thereby reducing the need for plea and charge bargaining as it is currently practiced. Bargaining might still be important, but it would be between criminals and victims, perhaps facilitated by a private mediator.

Implementing Punishment

The potential gains from contracting out for prisons clearly have not been exhausted. The relatively limited use of contract prisons reflects government barriers, rather than a lack of suppliers. For instance, Tennessee lawmakers turned down CCA's offer to take over the state's entire prison system, despite substantial cost savings. Furthermore, various states put tighter budgetary and/or operating restrictions on private prisons than on prisons built and operated by public agencies. These kinds of laws shelter state-run facilities and their employees from the forces of competition, thus undermining one of the potential benefits of privatization.[26]

Imprisonment is only one form of punishment, of course, and many of the alternatives are also contracted out (e.g., halfway houses and treatment programs).[27] However, two large pools of criminals are almost exclusively supervised by public employees: those on general probation and parole. And "to say that there are problems with both the probation and parole systems is putting it mildly" (Reynolds 1994, 30). After all, 38 percent of the people arrested for felonies are under criminal justice supervision in the form of parole, probation, or pretrial release (National Institute of Justice 1993). While parole and probation supervision have not been privatized, they quite easily could be, using the commercial bail system as a model (Reynolds 1994, 31).

Prisoners eligible for probation or parole could be required to post a financial bond, obtained for the most part from private bondsmen for a fee, against specified violations of their release program. Such a private financial market would provide valuable

---

26. A major source of political resistance to contracting out for prisons is organized correctional officers (Benson 1990: 334).

27. There are numerous "intermediate sanctions" between probation and imprisonment that may provide cost-effective alternatives to the prison/probation dichotomy, and many lend themselves to contracting. However, with the political-institutional environment that characterizes the public-sector criminal justice system, these alternatives tend to be underfunded and ineffectively utilized (Rasmussen and Benson 1994b).

information for the courts and parole boards: if bondsmen feel that a convicted felon is too risky to bond, then, as Reynolds (1994, 31) suggests, "why should the general public risk having that person on the street"? This would also substantially reduce the workload of public parole and probation officers since private bondsmen would provide close supervision in order to insure against loss of the bond, and a bounty hunter arrangement could easily develop to pursue those who flee, given that turning in such a fugitive would result in repayment of a substantial portion of the bond. If such privatization of probation and parole were to increase the effectiveness of selection and supervision, as private bail does relative to pretrial release, then the criminals released to these programs would pose lower threats to citizens.

Competitive Markets for Criminals' Labor

During the 19th century, many state prisons financed their own operations by selling prison labor or its products, even turning over surplus funds to state treasuries (Reynolds 1994, 33). Today, the prison population represents a huge pool of almost completely unused labor that simply drains state treasuries rather than contributing to them. Why? One answer is the inhumane treatment of prisoners in the historical prison work programs. However, these problems arose in facilities that monopolized prison labor.

Criminals could be protected against such abuses by having a choice between a specified prison term in a conventional state facility and voluntarily being supervised while working off a specified fine. Voluntary contracts could specify the work conditions and wages, and perhaps the portions of the wages going to pay off the fine, to "room and board," and to the prisoners' families (thereby reducing the welfare burden of the state as well). In fact, to further ensure against the dangers of abuse that characterized historical prison labor programs, the entire operation of the working prisons might be turned over to the private firms employing convicted criminals, and penal firms might bid for contracts from the state, assuming the risk of debt payment. Alternatively, the firms might bid competitively for contracts with offenders, who would then make payments to the state to cover the fines, and the contracts would be voidable if prisoners were abused. Competitive forces would work to preclude inhumane treatment of prisoners, as a firm with a reputation for mistreating prisoners clearly would not receive much business.

Would criminals actually voluntarily contract to work off their "debt"? Consider the results of a very limited prison work experiment. At the Maine State Prison, inmates were given access to the prison's shop equipment to produce novelties. Other prisons have done the same thing, but in Maine there is a strong market for novelties because the prison is located on a major tourist route. In addition, Maine inmates were allowed to hire one another, thus leading to efficiency-enhancing specialization and division of labor, and beginning in 1976, prisoners were allowed to "patent" their novelty designs, so they had incentives to innovate and expand their production. A "miniature economy" developed inside the prison, with two-thirds of the inmates acting as employers, employees, or both, even though prisoners could not use dollars for their labor market transactions (they used coupons that could be spent in the prison's canteen or banked in the prison's business office; Shedd 1982).

Clearly, prisoners will work voluntarily if incentives to do so exist, as they would if a prisoner could work off a predetermined fine. In fact, the sentence would have a self-determinative nature in that the harder a prisoner worked, the faster he or she could obtain release (Barnett 1977, 294).[28]

Barriers to Prison Work Programs

Prison industries were seen as "cheap labor" pools giving their employers unfair competitive advantages. Political opposition

---

28. The resulting incentives could have significant rehabilitative impacts (Barnett 1977: 293). Indeed, as Shedd (1982: 24) concluded, "It wasn't called that, but Maine State Prison had a rehabilitation program that was *working*." One novelty entrepreneur had 30 to 50 employees in novelty production, took over the prison's canteen, turned it into a profit-making operation, and diversified into other areas (e.g., he owned and rented about 100 TV sets to inmates; Shedd 1982: 26). After leaving prison, he opened a novelty firm employing former prisoners. There could be other benefits as well. For instance, "the convict will have a direct incentive to exhibit good behavior. The better risk he appears to the penal agency, the more likely he is to be allowed parole or other freedoms in the interest of increasing his productivity" (Sneed 1977: 123). Violence in prison probably would diminish. Even under the Maine novelty program, where greater freedoms were available, the major novelty producers used their economic power to "counteract theft...and general thuggism" because it threatened their enterprises (Shedd 1982: 27).

from both businesses and labor organizations resulted in state laws or constitutional provisions that prevent the sale of all but a few prison-made items (e.g., license plates).[29] Under similar pressure, Congress passed the Hawes-Cooper Act of 1935, prohibiting interstate commerce in prison-made products when the receiving state has laws against the marketing of such goods. Private firms were also prohibited from using prison labor under government contracts exceeding $10,000 by the Walsh-Healy Act of 1936. Then the 1940 Sumners-Ashurst Act made transport of prison-made goods across state borders illegal, regardless of state laws. As Shedd (1982, 27–28) explained:

> The effect of all these statutes was virtually to wipe out the market for prisoner labor and for prisoner-made goods....[I]n virtually every prison the only work opportunities are in the traditional prison industries—the making of license plates being, of course, the classic example—and in prison maintenance and custodial work. In almost every case these positions are low-paying, and in spite of that the industries involved are almost everywhere money losers.

Thus, while self-supported, privately run prisons, with humane treatment of prisoners established through competitive labor markets, are both feasible and desirable, they will not develop without repeal of statutes limiting the market for prison-made goods.

The timing may be ripe for repeal of these laws, however, as prison costs are soaring and evidence is mounting that prison work programs can be developed to the satisfaction of both prisoners and public officials. In fact, a number of experimental

---

29. Other political interests may also be important. For instance, on April 16, 1980, a lockdown of the Maine State Prison began, and an extensive search and seizure operation destroyed the prisoners' businesses. After the lockdown, substantial reductions in economic rights and incentives were implemented, destroying any potential for reviving the program. Why? One explanation may be that for several years, the Maine Corrections Bureau had tried unsuccessfully to obtain larger budgets and to have the bureau elevated to cabinet level. Following the lockdown, key legislators switched their position on both issues. Another explanation may simply be bureaucratic rigidity and resistance to change: prison authorities wanted complete control over prisoners, not "ambitious and talented individuals finding a way around bureaucratic restrictions on their activities" (Shedd 1982: 9). This is one reason to expect that prison work programs will have greater success in private prisons.

"exceptions" to statutory restrictions have been granted in recent years, after consulting with labor-union officials and guaranteeing that prisoners would be paid the prevailing wage (something that would characterize a competitive market for prison labor), that other workers would not be adversely affected, and that the resulting product would not compete in an industry currently experiencing local unemployment. A 1989 National Institute of Justice survey identified more than 70 private manufacturing, service, and light-assembly firms that employed prison labor in 16 states (Stewart 1989).

PRIDE, a state-sponsored private corporation, runs 46 prison industries in Florida, and South Carolina and Nevada are leaders in developing private-sector use of prison labor. South Carolina prisoners in the start-up phase of two private-sector programs had earned $2.4 million by the end of 1992, for example, with about $500,000 going to taxes, $119,000 to victim compensation, $322,000 to room and board, $364,000 to families, and $1.1 million to inmate savings (Reynolds 1994, 34).

Restitution and Private Collections

The federal government began supporting some short-term restitution program experiments in 1978. Poole (1980, 1) described an example:

> When "Fred Stone" broke into the Tucson house and stole the color TV, he had little idea that he would be caught. Still less did he expect to be confronted face-to-face by the victim, in the county prosecutor's office. In the course of the meeting, Stone learned that the TV set was the center of the elderly, invalid woman's life. With the approval of the Pima County, Arizona, prosecutor, he agreed not only to return the TV, but also to paint her house, mow her lawn, and drive her to the doctor for her weekly checkup. By doing so he avoided a jail sentence, and saved Tucson area taxpayers several thousand dollars.

Poole makes three important points here. First, even though sanctioned by public prosecutors and courts, some restitution programs have found it desirable to mediate private restitution contracts between the offender and the victim (Poole 1977, 1; Anderson 1983). Thus, the prosecutor and court become an arbitrator-mediator, clearly a service that could be privatized.

Second, restitution need not be monetary. One criticism of monetary fines is that criminals may be judgment proof because they are unable to pay a fine large enough to either compensate the victim or be an effective deterrent. However, criminals should be allowed to work off their restitution, either by working directly for the victim or by selling labor, perhaps in a prison environment. "Community service" sentences seem to be popular in many states today for various misdemeanors and minor felonies. Why not "victim service" sentences?

Third, restitution is a relatively efficient form of punishment (Friedman 1979, 408; Barnett 1977, 29). Imprisonment wastes tremendous amounts of resources in the form of idle prisoners' time. Even if close supervision in prison work programs is required to ensure restitution payments, prisoners are working to produce goods for sale rather than being idle.

Refocusing the criminal justice system to emphasize restitution means that the restitution payment process could be specified contractually. If a victim perceives a risk of reneging, a private "collection" agency could be employed to supervise the contract, providing the necessary level of monitoring and security to see that payments are made. This is not very different from a restitution program called EARN-IT, in Quincy County, Massachusetts, where 40 local businesses provided jobs to offenders who were unable to find jobs elsewhere (Anderson 1983, 27). The employers acted as supervisors during work hours, and the offenders reported to probation officers.

In other experimental restitution programs, offenders returned to jail or a halfway house at night (recall that most halfway houses are contracted out to private firms, which clearly could also collect and distribute restitution payments). If the risk of reneging is large enough, private firms employing prison labor could serve as collection agencies. Indeed, such a firm might pay a bond to the victim equal to the discounted value of the anticipated restitution and then collect the payments itself in order to recover the bond plus interest.

For the imposition of punishment, as for increasing the probability of reporting, arrest, prosecution, and conviction, refocusing criminal justice on restitution for victims would create many more opportunities for cost-effective privatization. In fact, the full potential for privatization cannot be achieved, or probably even envisioned, without a reorientation of criminal justice toward concern for victims: the people who should be the most important "customers" in the market for justice.

Conclusions

A large number of privatization options have been discussed, from more contracting out, to lifting legal barriers that limit the use of private security, to a major reorientation of criminal justice into a restitution-based system that allows private courts (arbitrators or mediators) to determine restitution fines and private prison firms to collect them. If governments do not follow at least some of these recommendations, privatization will occur to a large degree anyway (Benson 1990). After all, the growth in private security, protection, and justice documented above has occurred in the face of the legal barriers that are the focus of several of the recommendations made here. Legal barriers can prevent some cost-effective privatization (private markets for criminal labor, private prosecution, formal private criminal courts, etc.), and they can slow the process and divert its path, perhaps in undesirable ways (e.g., creating incentives for the secretive application of destructive and/or violent private justice), but it is too late to halt the process. Therefore, as an alternative, government officials should seriously consider supporting and even encouraging privatization, thereby perhaps influencing some of the inevitable developments.

References

Anderson, David C. 1983. EARN-IT: A Key to the Prison Dilemma. *Across the Board* 20 (November): 34-42.

Auerbach, Jerold S. 1983. *Justice Without Law?* New York: Oxford University Press.

Barnett, Randy E. 1977. Restitution: A New Paradigm of Criminal Justice. *Ethics* 87 (July).

———. 1984. Public Decisions and Private Rights. *Criminal Justice Ethics* (Summer/Fall): 50-62.

Beck, Allen J. 1987. Recidivism of Young Parolees. *Special Report.* Washington, D.C.: U.S. Department of Justice, Bureau of Justice Statistics, May.

Benson, Bruce L. 1981. A Note on Corruption of Public Officials: The Black Market for Property Rights. *Journal of Libertarian Studies* 5 (Summer): 305-11.

———. 1990. *The Enterprise of Law: Justice Without the State.* San Francisco: Pacific Research Institute for Public Policy.

———. 1994a. Are Public Goods Really Common Pools: Considerations of the Evolution of Policing and Highways in England. *Economic Inquiry* 32 (April): 249-71.

———. 1994b. Third Thoughts on Contracting Out. *Journal of Libertarian Studies* 11 (Fall): 44-78.

———. 1995. An Exploration of the Impact of Modern Arbitration Statutes on the Development of Arbitration in the United States. *Journal of Law, Economics, and Organization* 11 (October): 479-501.

———. Forthcoming. Toxic Torts by Government. In *Toxic Liability: Tort Law, Bureaucracy, and the Environment,* edited by R. Stroup and R. Meiners. Oakland, Calif.: The Independent Institute.

Benson, Bruce L., and David W. Rasmussen. 1994. *Crime in Florida.* Tallahassee, Report to the Florida Chamber of Commerce, March.

Bottom, Norman K., and John Kostanoski. 1983 *Security and Loss Control.* New York: Macmillan.

Bowman, Gary W., Simon Hakim, and Paul Seidenstat, eds. 1993. *Privatizing Correctional Institutions.* New Brunswick, N.J.: Transaction.

Bureau of Census. Various years. *County Business Patterns.* Washington D.C.: U.S. Department of Commerce, Bureau of Census.

Bureau of Justice Statistics (BJS). 1990. *Pretrial Release of Felony Defendants.* Washington D.C.: U.S. Department of Justice, Bureau of Justice Statistics.

———. 1993. *Highlights from 20 Years of Surveying Crime Victims: The National Victimization Survey, 1973-1992.* Washington, D.C.: U.S. Department of Justice, Office of Justice Programs, October.

California Department of Justice. 1981. *Homicide in California, 1981.* Sacramento: Bureau of Criminal Statistics and Special Services.

Cardenas, Juan. 1986.The Crime Victim in the Prosecutional Process. *Harvard Journal of Law and Public Policy* (Spring): 357-98.

Chaiken, Marcia, and Jan Chaiken. 1987. *Public Policing—Privately Provided.* Washington, D.C.: U.S. Department of Justice, National Institute of Justice.

Clotfelter, Charles T. 1977. Public Services, Private Substitutes, and the Demand for Protection Against Crime. *American Economic Review* 67 (December).

Criminal Justice Associates. 1990. *Private Sector Prison Industries.* Philadelphia: Criminal Justice Associates, December 7.

Cunningham, William C., and Todd H. Taylor. 1985 *Crime and Protection in America: A Study of Private Security and Law Enforcement Resources and Relationships.* Washington D.C.: U.S. Department of Justice, National Institute of Justice.

Cunningham, William C., John J. Strauchs and Clifford W. Van Meter. 1991. Private Security: Patterns and Trends. *National Institute of Justice: Research in Brief* (August).

Denenberg, Tai Schneider, and R.V. Denenberg. 1981. *Dispute Resolution: Settling Conflicts Without Legal Action.* Public Affairs Pamphlet No. 597. New York: Public Affairs Committee, Inc.

Dewhurst, H. S. 1955. *The Railroad Police.* Springfield, Ill.: Charles C. Thomas, Publishers.

Dobson, Christopher, and Ronald Payne. 1983. Private Enterprise Takes on Terrorism. *Reason* 14 (January).

Donovan, Edwin J., and William F. Walsh. 1986. *An Evaluation of Starrett City Security Services.* University Park: Penn State Univ.

Dorffi, Christine. 1979. San Francisco's Hired Guns. *Reason* (August).

Ellickson, Robert C. 1991. *Order Without Law: How Neighbors Settle Disputes.* Cambridge, Mass.: Harvard University Press.

Fisk, Donald; Herbert Kiesling, and Thomas Muller. 1978. *Private Provision of Public Services: An Overview.* Washington D.C.: Urban Institute.

Fitch, Lyle C. 1974. Increasing the Role of the Private Sector in Providing Public Services. In *Improving the Quality of Urban Management*, edited by Willis D. Hawley and David Rogers, vol. 8 of *Urban Affairs Annual Review.* Beverly Hills, Calif.: Sage.

Fixler, Philip E. Jr. 1984. Can Privatization Solve the Prison Crisis? *Fiscal Watchdog* 90 (April).

Florestano, Patricia S., and Stephen B. Gordon. 1980. Public vs. Private: Small Government Contracting with the Private Sector. *Public Administration Review* 40 (January/February).

Friedman, David. 1979. Private Creation and Enforcement of Law: A Historical Case. *Journal of Legal Studies* 8 (March): 399–415.

Gage, Theodore J. 1981. Getting Street-Wise in St. Louis. *Reason* (August).

———. 1982. Cops, Inc. *Reason* 14 (March).

Granelli, James S. 1981.Got a Spat? Go Rent a Judge. *National Law Journal* (June 8).

Hannan, Timothy. 1982. Bank Robberies and Bank Security Precautions. *Journal of Legal Studies* 11 (January).

Henry, Stuart. 1987.Private Justice and the Policing of Labor: The Dialectic of Industrial Discipline. In *Private Police*, edited by C. Shearing and P. Stenning. Newbury Park, Calif.: Sage.

Hensler, Deborah R., Mary E. Vaina, James S. Kakalik, and Mark A. Peterson. 1987. *Trends in Tort Litigation: The Story Behind the Statistics.* Santa Monica, Calif.: Rand Institute for Civil Justice.

Iwata, Edward. 1984 Rent-a-Cops on Trial. *This World* (March 18).

Joel, Dana C. 1993. The Privatization of Secure Adult Prisons: Issues and Evidence. In *Privatizing Correctional Institutions*, edited by Gary W. Bowman, S. Hakim, and P. Seidenstat. New Brunswick, N.J.: Transaction.

Jones, David. 1979. *Crime Without Punishment.* Lexington, Mass.: Lexington Books.

Kakalik, James S., and Sorrel Wildhorn. 1971. *Private Police in the United States: Findings and Recommendations.* Santa Monica, Calif.: Rand Corporation.

Kleck, Gary, and David Bordua. 1983. The Factual Foundation for Certain Key Assumptions of Gun Control. *Law and Policy Quarterly* 5 (Spring): 271-98.

Klein, S., and M. Caggiano. 1986. *The Prevalence, Predictability, and Policy Implications of Recidivism.* Santa Monica, Calif.: Rand Corporation.

Krajick, Kevin. 1984a. Private, For-Profit Prisons Take Hold in Some States. *Christian Science Monitor* (April 11).

———. 1984b. Punishment for Profit. *Across the Board* 21 (March).

Landes, William M. 1974.Legality and Reality: Some Evidence of Criminal Procedure. *Journal of Legal Studies* (June).

Lawrence, Richard. 1991. The Impact of Sentencing Guidelines on Corrections. Paper presented at the annual meeting of the Academy of Criminal Justice Sciences.

Lazarus, Steven, John J. Bray Jr., Larry L. Carter, Kent H. Collins, Bruce A. Giedt, Robert V. Holton Jr., Phillip D. Matthews, and Gordon C. Willard. 1965. *Resolving Business Disputes: The Potential for Commercial Arbitration.* New York: American Management Association.

Logan, Charles H. 1990. *Private Prisons: Cons and Pros.* New York: Oxford University Press.

———. 1992. Well Kept: Comparing Quality of Confinement in Private and Public Prisons. *Journal of Criminal Law and Criminology* 83 (Fall): 577-613.

Logan, Charles H., and Bill W. McGriff. 1989. Comparing Costs of Public and Private Prisons: A Case Study. *National Institute of Justice: Research in Review* (September/October).

Logan, Charles H., Shardla P. Rausch. 1985 Punish and Profit: The Emergence of Private Enterprise Prisons. *Justice Quarterly* 2 (September): 303-18.

Lott, John R. Jr. 1987. Should the Wealthy Be Able to 'Buy Justice'? *Journal of Political Economy* 95 (December): 1307-16.

Marx, Gary T., and Dane Archer. 1971. Citizen Involvement in the Law Enforcement Process: The Case of Community Police Patrols. *American Behavioral Scientist* 15: 52-72.

McDonald, William F. 1977. The Role of the Victim in America. In *Assessing the Criminal: Restitution and the Legal Process,* edited by Randy E. Barnett and John Hagel III, Cambridge, Mass.: Ballinger.

McGrath, Roger D. 1984. *Gunfighters, Highwaymen, and Vigilantes: Violence on the Frontier.* Berkeley: University of California Press.

Meiners, Roger E. 1977. Public Compensation of the Victims of Crime: How Much Would it Cost? In *Assessing the Criminal: Restitution, Retribution, and the Legal Process,* edited by Randy E. Barnett and John Hagel III. Cambridge, Mass.: Ballinger.

Miller, Rod, George E.Sexton, and Victor J. Jacobsen. 1991. *Making Jails Productive.* Washington, D.C.: U.S. Department of Justice, National Institute of Justice, October.

Monks, Gerald P. 1986. Public Bail—A National Disaster. In *Crime and Punishment in Modern America*, edited by Patrick B. McGuigan and Jon S. Pascale. Washington D.C.: Institute for Government and Politics of the Free Congress Research and Education Foundation.

Mullen, Joan, Kent Chabotar, and Deborah Carrow. 1985. *The Privatization of Corrections.* Abt Associates report to the National Institute of Justice. Washington D.C.: U.S. Department of Justice, February.

National Advisory Commission on Criminal Justice Standards and Goals. 1973. *Report on Police.* Washington, D.C.: U.S. Department of Justice, Law Enforcement Assistance Administration.

———. 1976. *Private Security: Report of the Task Force on Private Security.* Washington D.C.: U.S. Department of Justice, Law Enforcement Assistance Administration.

National Institute of Justice 1993. *Felony Defendants in Large Urban Counties, 1990.* Washington, D.C.: U.S. Department of Justice, National Institute of Justice, May.

Neely, Richard. 1982. *Why Courts Don't Work.* New York: McGraw-Hill.

Newman, Oscar. 1980. *Community of Interest.* Garden City, N.Y.: Anchor Press.

New York Times. 1980. Private Everything. October 20, p. D3.

Phalon, Richard. 1992. Privatizing Justice. *Forbes* (December 7): 126–27.

Podolefsky, Aaron, and Fredric Dubow. 1981. *Strategies for Community Crime Prevention: Collective Responses to Crime in Urban America.* Springfield, Ill.: Charles C. Thomas, Publisher.

Poole, Robert W. Jr. 1977. More Justice—For Less Money. *Fiscal Watchdog* (July).

———. 1978. *Cutting Back City Hall.* New York: Free Press.

———. 1980. Can Justice Be Privatized? *Fiscal Watchdog* 49 (November).

———. 1983. Rehabilitating the Correctional System. *Fiscal Watchdog* 81 (July).

Predicasts, Inc. 1970. *Special Study 56.* Predicasts, Inc., March 5.

Pruitt, Gary. 1982.California's Rent-a-Judge Justice. *Journal of Contemporary Studies* 5 (Spring): 49–57.

Pudlow, Jan. 1993. Without Restitution, Crime Really Does Pay. (January 3) E1 and E4. *Tallahassee Democrat.*

Rasmussen, David W., and Bruce L. Benson. 1994a. *The Economic Anatomy of a Drug War: Criminal Justice in the Commons.* Lanham, Md.: Rowman and Littlefield.

———. 1994b. *Intermediate Sanctions: A Policy Analysis Based on Program Evaluations.* Report to the Florida Task Force for the Review of the Criminal Justice and Corrections Systems. Tallahassee, September.

Reaves, Brian A. 1992a. Sheriff's Departments. 1990 *Bureau of Justice Statistics Bulletin* (February): 1–11.

——. 1992b. State and Local Police Departments. *Bureau of Justice Statistics Bulletin* (February): 11–14.

Reichman, Nancy. 1987. The Widening Webs of Surveillance: Private Police Unraveling Deceptive Claims. In *Private Policing,* edited by Clifford D. Shearing and Philip C. Stenning. Newbury Park, Calif.: Sage.

Research and Forecasts, Inc. 1983. *America Afraid: How Fear of Crime Changes the Way We Live, Based on the Widely Publicized Figgie Report.* New York: New America Library.

Reynolds, Morgan O. 1994. *Using the Private Sector to Deter Crime.* Dallas, Tex.: National Center for Policy Analysis.

Ricks, Truett A., Bill G. Tillett, and Clifford W. Van Meter. 1981. *Principles of Security.* Cincinnati: Criminal Justice Studies, Anderson Publishing.

Savas, E. S. 1974.Municipal Monopolies Versus Competition in Delivering Urban Services. In *Improving the Quality of Urban Management*, edited by Willis D. Hawley and David Rogers, vol. 8 of *Urban Affairs Annual Review.* Beverly Hills, Calif.: Sage.

Schulhofer, Stephen J. 1988. Criminal Justice Discretion as a Regulatory System. *Journal of Legal Studies* 17 (January): 43–82.

Schulhofer, Stephen J., and David D. Friedman. 1993. Rethinking Indigent Defense: Promoting Effective Representation Through Consumer Sovereignty and Freedom of Choice for All Criminals. *American Criminal Law Review* 31 (Fall): 73–122.

Shearing, Clifford D., and Phillip C. Stenning. 1987. Say Cheese! The Disney Order That Is Not So Mickey Mouse. In *Private Policing*, edited by C. Shearing and P. Stenning. Newbury Park, Calif.: Sage.

Shedd, Jeffrey. 1982. Making Good[s] Behind Bars. *Reason* 13 (March).

Sherman, Lawrence W. 1983. Patrol Strategies for Police. In *Crime and Public Policy*, edited by J. Wilson. San Francisco: Institute for Contemporary Studies.

Skogan, Wesley, and Michael Maxfield. 1979. *Coping with Crime: Victimization, Fear, and Reaction to Crime in Three American Cities.* Evanston, Ill.: Center for Urban Studies, Northwestern University.

Skolnick, Jerome, and David H. Bayley. 1988. Theme and Variation in Community Policing. In *Crime and Justice: A Review of Research*, edited by M. Tonry and N. Morris. Chicago: University of Chicago Press.

Sneed, John. 1977. Order Without Law: Where Will the Anarchists Keep the Madman? *Journal of Libertarian Studies* 1.

Sorin, Martin D. 1986. *Out on Bail.* Washington, D.C.: U.S. Department of Justice, National Institute of Justice.

Stewart, George R. 1964. *Committee of Vigilance: Revolution in San Francisco, 1851.* Boston: Houghton Mifflin.

Stewart, James K. 1989. Letter from James K. Stewart (director of the National Institute of Justice) to the *Wall Street Journal,* July 26.

Stigler, George J. 1971. The Theory of Economic Regulation. *Bell Journal of Economics and Management Science* 2 (Spring): 3-21.

Trojanowicz, Robert, and Mark H. Moore. 1988. *The Meaning of Community in Community Policing.* East Lansing, Mich.: National Neighborhood Foot Patrol Center.

Tullock, Gordon. 1970. *Private Wants, Public Means: An Economic Analysis of the Desirable Scope of Government.* New York: Basic Books.

U.S. News and World Report. 1983. Private Police Forces in Growing Demand. January 29, pp. 54-56.

Valentine, Alan. 1956. *Vigilante Justice.* New York: Reynal and Co.

Wilson, James Q. 1977. Thinking Practically About Crime. In *Assessing the Criminal: Restitution, Retribution, and the Legal Process,* edited by Randy E. Barnett and John Hagel III. Cambridge, Mass.: Ballinger.

Wilson, Richard J. 1982. *Contract Bid Program: A Threat to Quality Indigent Care.* National Legal Aid and Defender Association.

Wooldridge, William C. 1970. *Uncle Sam, The Monopoly Man.* New Rochelle, N.Y.: Arlington House.

Wynne, John M. Jr. 1978. *Prison Employee Unionism: The Impact on Correctional Administration and Programs.* Washington, D.C.: National Institute of Law Enforcement and Criminal Justice, January.

Yin, Robert K., Mary E. Vogel, Jan N. Chaiken, and Deborah R. Both. 1977. *Citizen Patrol Projects.* Washington, D.C.: National Institute of Law Enforcement and Criminal Justice, Law Enforcement Assistance Administration, U.S. Department of Justice.

THE INDEPENDENT INSTITUTE is a non-profit, non-partisan, scholarly research and educational organization which sponsors comprehensive studies on the political economy of critical social and economic problems.

The politicization of decision-making in society has largely confined public debate to the narrow reconsideration of existing policies. Given the prevailing influence of partisan interests, little social innovation has occurred. In order to understand both the nature of and possible solutions to major public issues, The Independent Institute's program adheres to the highest standards of independent inquiry and is pursued regardless of prevailing political or social biases and conventions. The resulting studies are widely distributed as books and other publications, and publicly debated through numerous conference and media programs.

Through this uncommon independence, depth, and clarity, the Independent Institute pushes at the frontiers of our knowledge, redefines the debate over public issues, and fosters new and effective directions for government reform.

FOUNDER & PRESIDENT
David J. Theroux

RESEARCH DIRECTOR
Robert Higgs, Ph.D.

ACADEMIC ADVISORS
Stephen E. Ambrose
University of New Orleans
Martin Anderson
Hoover Institution
Herman Belz
University of Maryland
Thomas E. Borcherding
Claremont Graduate School
Boudewijn Bouckaert
University of Ghent, Belgium
James M. Buchanan
Center for the Study of Public Choice, George Mason University
Allan C. Carlson
Rockford Institute
Robert W. Crandall
Brookings Institution
Stephen J. DeCanio
University of California, Santa Barbara
Arthur A. Ekirch, Jr.
State University of New York, Albany
Richard A. Epstein
University of Chicago
B. Delworth Gardner
Brigham Young University

George Gilder
Discovery Institute
Nathan Glazer
Harvard University
Ronald Hamowy
University of Alberta
Steve H. Hanke
Johns Hopkins University
Ronald Max Hartwell
Oxford University
Deirdre N. McCloskey
University of Iowa
J. Huston McCulloch
Ohio State University
Forrest McDonald
University of Alabama
Merton H. Miller
University of Chicago
Thomas Gale Moore
Hoover Institution
Charles Murray
American Enterprise Institute
William A. Niskanen
Cato Institute
Michael J. Novak, Jr.
American Enterprise Institute
Charles E. Phelps
University of Rochester
Paul Craig Roberts
Institute for Political Economy
Nathan Rosenberg
Stanford University

Simon Rottenberg
University of Massachusetts
Bruce M. Russett
Yale University
Pascal Salin
University of Paris, France
Arthur Seldon
Institute of Economic Affairs, England
Julian L. Simon
University of Maryland
Joel H. Spring
State University of New York, Old Westbury
Richard L. Stroup
Montana State University
Thomas S. Szasz
State University of New York, Syracuse
Robert D. Tollison
George Mason University
Arnold S. Trebach
American University
Gordon Tullock
University of Arizona
Richard E. Wagner
George Mason University
Sir Alan A. Walters
AIG Trading Corporation
Carolyn L. Weaver
American Enterprise Institute
Walter E. Williams
George Mason University

INDEPENDENT STUDIES IN POLITICAL ECONOMY

THE ACADEMY IN CRISIS: *The Political Economy of Higher Education.* Edited by John W. Sommer, foreword by Nathan Glazer, 348 pages, $34.95 hc, $19.95 pb.

AGRICULTURE AND THE STATE: *Market Processes and Bureaucracy.* E. C. Pasour, Jr., foreword by Bruce L. Gardner, 288 pages, $39.95 hc, $19.95 pb.

ALIENATION AND THE SOVIET ECONOMY: *The Collapse of the Socialist Era.* Paul Craig Roberts, foreword by Aaron Wildavsky, 152 pages, $29.95 hc, $16.95 pb.

ANTITRUST AND MONOPOLY: *Anatomy of A Policy Failure.* D. T. Armentano, foreword by Yale Brozen, 312 pages, $19.95 pb.

ARMS, POLITICS AND THE ECONOMY: *Historical and Contemporary Perspectives.* Edited by Robert Higgs, foreword by William A. Niskanen, 328 pages, $44.95 hc, $19.95 pb.

BEYOND POLITICS: *Markets, Welfare, and the Failure of Bureaucracy.* William C. Mitchell and Randy T. Simmons, foreword by Gordon Tullock, 256 pages, $49.95 hc, $17.95 pb.

THE DIVERSITY MYTH: *"Multiculturalism" and the Politics of Intolerance at Stanford.* David O. Sacks and Peter A. Thiel, foreword by Elizabeth Fox-Genovese, 312 pages, $24.95 hc.

FREEDOM, FEMINISM AND THE STATE. Edited by Wendy McElroy, foreword by Lewis Perry, 272 pages, $49.95 hc, $19.95 pb.

HAZARDOUS TO OUR HEALTH? *FDA Regulation of Health Care Products.* Edited by Robert Higgs, foreword by Joel J. Nobel, 128 pages, $14.95 pb.

OUT OF WORK: *Unemployment and Government in Twentieth-Century America.* Richard K. Vedder and Lowell E. Gallaway, foreword by Martin Bronfenbrenner, 352 pages, $34.95 hc, $16.95 pb.

PRIVATE RIGHTS AND PUBLIC ILLUSIONS. Tibor R. Machan, foreword by Nicholas Rescher, 408 pages, $34.95 hc, $19.95 pb.

REGULATION AND THE REAGAN ERA: *Politics, Bureaucracy and the Public Interest.* Edited by Roger E. Meiners and Bruce Yandle, Jr., foreword by Robert W. Crandall, 320 pages, $49.95 hc, $19.95 pb.

TAXING ENERGY: *Oil Severance Taxation and the Economy.* Robert Deacon, Stephen Decanio, H. E. Frech, III, and M. Bruce Johnson, foreword by Joseph P. Kalt, 176 pages, $39.95 hc.

THAT EVERY MAN BE ARMED: *The Evolution of a Constitutional Right.* Stephen P. Halbrook, 274 pages, $49.95 hc, $16.95 pb.

Books in Preparation:

AMERICAN HEALTH CARE: *Government, Markets, and Public Interest.* Edited by Robert Higgs and Simon Rottenberg.

CAPITALIST REVOLUTION IN LATIN AMERICA. Paul Craig Roberts and Karen L. Araujo, foreword by Lord Peter T. Bauer.

CRIMINAL JUSTICE: *The Private Challenge to Crime Reduction and Prevention.* Bruce L. Benson.

MONEY AND THE NATION STATE. *The Financial Revolution, Government and the World Monetary System.* Edited by Richard H. Timberlake, Jr. and Kevin Dowd, foreword by Merton H. Miller.

POLITICAL ECOLOGY: *Bureaucracy, Myths, and Endangered Species.* Randy Simmons and Charles Kay.

TAXING CHOICE: *The Predatory Politics of Fiscal Discrimination.* Edited by William F. Shughart II, foreword by Paul W. McCracken.

THE VOLUNTARY CITY: *New Directions for Urban America.* Edited by David T. Beito.

TOXIC LIABILITY: *Tort Law, Bureaucracy, and the Environment.* Edited by Roger E. Meiners and Richard L. Stroup.

INDEPENDENT POLICY REPORTS

FREEDOM OF CONTRACT: *The Unexplored Path to Health Care Reform.* Clark C. Havighurst, 32 pages, $5.95.

WEALTH CREATION AS A "SIN". Jonathan R. Macey, 32 pages, $5.95.

ANTIDISCRIMINATION IN HEALTH CARE: *Community Ratings and Pre-Existing Conditions.* Richard A. Epstein, 36 pages, $5.95.

ILLICIT DRUGS AND CRIME. Bruce L. Benson and David W. Rasmussen, 64 pages, $7.95.

CULTURE AND CRIME. Allan Carlson and Christopher Check, 48 pages, $6.95.

VICTIMS' RIGHTS, RESTITUTION, AND RETRIBUTION. Williamson M. Evers, 52 pages, $7.95.

POLICE SERVICES: *The Private Challenge.* Erwin Blackstone and Simon Hakim, 44 pages, $6.95.

CIVIL FORFEITURE AS A "SIN" TAX. Donald J. Boudreaux and Adam C. Pritchard, 32 pages, $5.95.

BANK DEPOSIT GUARANTEES: Why Not Trust the Market? Genie D. Short and Kenneth J. Robinson, 40 pages, $6.95.

TOXIC TORTS BY GOVERNMENT. Bruce L. Benson, 52 pages, $6.95.

REGULATION OF CARCINOGENS: Are Animal Tests a Sound Foundation? Aaron Wildavsky, 44 pages, $6.95.

PROPAGANDA OF THE "NANNY STATE." Thomas J. DiLorenzo, 37 pages, $4.95.

SUPERFUND AND RISKY RISK REDUCTION. Bruce M. Yandle, 35 pages, $5.95.

PRIVATIZATION IN CRIMINAL JUSTICE. Bruce L. Benson, 68 pages, $7.95.

WOLF RECOVERY, POLITICAL ECOLOGY, AND ENDANGERED SPECIES. Charles Kay, 35 pages, $5.95.

FIREARMS AND CRIME. Daniel D. Polsby, 38 pages, $5.95.

PRISONS AND CORRECTIONS. Samuel Jan Brakel and Bruce L. Benson, 67 pages, $7.95.

MONETARY NATIONALISM RECONSIDERED. Lawrence H. White, 36 pages, $6.95.

CRIME AND WELFARE. Richard E. Wagner, *in preparation.*

THE INDEPENDENT REVIEW

The INDEPENDENT REVIEW: A Journal of Political Economy, edited by Robert Higgs, Research Director for The Independent Institute, is an interdisciplinary, quarterly journal that features comprehensive studies of the political economy of critical public issues and includes book reviews, figures, tables, and an annual index. *The INDEPENDENT REVIEW* comprises approximately 600 pages per volume, and subscriptions are $27.95 per year for individuals and $49.95 per year for institutions. International subscribers add $28.00 for shipping and handling.

For further information and a catalog of publications, please contact:

THE INDEPENDENT INSTITUTE

134 Ninety-Eighth Avenue, Oakland, CA 94603
(510) 632-1366, fax: (510) 568-6040, E-mail orders@independent.org.